Experiencing
WOODLAND
POND

A PERSONAL HISTORY OF LAUGHING, LEARNING, LOVING AND LIVING IN A CONTINUING CARE RETIREMENT COMMUNITY

RICHARD V. BARRY

Winterlight Books

Shelbyville, KY USA

Experiencing Woodland Pond
by Richard V. Barry

First Printing – September 2013
ISBN: 978-1-60047-908-3

Printed in the U.S.A.

0   1   2   3   4   5   6   7   8   9   10   11

BOOKS BY RICHARD V. BARRY

Short Stories

CROSSCURRENTS: Stories of People in Conflict

PERSONAL WARS

INFINITE GESTURES

Novels

AN INCONVENIENT DEATH

QUALITIES OF MERCY

IN EVIL'S VORTEX

Novella

HISTORY OF THE SMILING YOUNG LORD

DEDICATION

TO all my new friends at Woodland Pond whose warm, supportive fellowship I treasure;

TO Robert Seidman whose leadership I admire;

As always, TO Katy who encouraged me to write this personal history;

FINALLY, TO all the citizens of this much-loved community, bonded in caring for one another.

"TO laugh often and much; to win the respect of intelligent people and the affection of children; to earn the appreciation of honest critics and endure the betrayal of false friends; to appreciate beauty; to find the best in others; to leave the world a bit better, whether by a healthy child, a garden patch, or a redeemed social condition; to know even one life has breathed easier because you have lived. This is to have succeeded."

-Ralph Waldo Emerson

NOTE: References to specific residents in this history have been made with their gracious permission.

SPECIAL THANKS to Anne Hanover and Vivian Moscowitz for applying their meticulous proofreading skills to this book in manuscript form.

Table of Contents

Experiencing
WOODLAND
POND

FOREWORD

This is a love story! Having stated that, I should explain that it's not a romantic tale as most people might automatically assume. But, as we know, love comes in many forms and variations and love plays a major role in these pages—love in the sense of a strong emotional attachment. I don't consider it unmanly to state that in coming to the community of Woodland Pond at New Paltz at the mature age of seventy-four, I fell in love with its natural setting, its amenities, its programs and, more importantly, its residents and professional staff.

Woodland Pond is, by any standard, a special community. I have been a resident here for two years. In that time I have never known a period of greater contentment, a persistent state of happiness bordering on giddy euphoria, as well as a period of greater productivity in my (second) career as a writer. I have to pinch myself frequently as a reminder that all this is true and how lucky I am! Only in hindsight, however, do I realize what a considerable gamble I took, a leap of faith, in choosing Woodland Pond as my last community—by actual count this is my twenty-third residence; fortunately that gamble has paid off in rich dividends and unexpected rewards.

With new longevity rates and an exploding population of senior citizens, varieties of senior establishments have proliferated to meet our needs. They can range from gated communities with minimum-age entrance requirements to assisted living facilities, to skilled nursing-care homes. Depending on one's state of health, frame of mind and economic circumstances, a senior can choose from a multiplicity of offerings. But, as I discovered, only a Continuing Care Retirement Community (CCRC), such as Woodland Pond, can offer the security and comfort of allowing a person to choose a designated community where

you can live independently and then, as health needs change, seamlessly move into adjacent quarters where greater care is provided, without leaving your familiar surroundings and solicitous friends.

Like any neighborhood or housing complex, each community has a style, a culture that determines the rhythm and flow of any day. The residents, of course, in their attitudes, interests and pursuits, indelibly shape the predominant culture. In this area alone, no brochure or marketing tool can fully delineate what the prevailing culture and the nuances of that culture are until one experiences it first-hand.

To my great delight—and considerable relief—I discovered upon my first days of residency that my new community was an active and vital population of vibrant people spanning a broad spectrum of ethnic, cultural and political backgrounds. In bringing a wealth of professional and personal experience to the enjoyment of their retirement years, they eagerly pursue artistic and intellectual interests while remaining fully connected to the larger world of politics, trends and world events.

Doctors, nurses, psychologists, social workers, professional artists, lawyers, ministers, hoteliers, business men and women, both corporate and entrepreneurial, professors, teachers, guidance counselors, librarians, school administrators, engineers and civic leaders—all form a rich tapestry of backgrounds that enlivens our communal life. Consequently, this is a community infused with spirited discussions, abundant laughter, variegated learning and, yes, a bond of loving friendships and manifold acts of kindness.

One of the first lessons I learned upon my arrival at my new residence was that appearances can be deceptive. Perhaps we don't walk with the briskness of our youth and maybe we find devices such as hearing aids or canes to be helpful, but that doesn't impede our zest for living. In squarely facing the challenges of advancing years and accommodating their lifestyles to any developing physical challenges, without losing

their positive perspective and *joie de vivre,* the residents of Woodland Pond quickly became, for me, models of how to grow older gracefully, with courage and undaunted spirit.

I like to think that as we mature, we develop the ability to see things more clearly and to eschew all pretenses. At Woodland Pond, candor and straightforwardness are hallmarks of our population. I learned this firsthand shortly after my arrival when dinner conversations often included a person's casual but proud reference to his or her age—so different from the prevailing national culture where youth is worshipped and the normal advancement of years is resisted if not completely denied. As a matter of fact, aging and its attendant physical challenges were frequently the subject of self-deprecating jokes. Many other references in conversations reinforced the pleasurable observation that my fellow residents forthrightly confronted all the realities of longevity with their dignity and sense of humor intact. I quickly learned to look beyond the physical appearance and relish the spirit within.

Scientists claim that the major contributing factors to a long and healthy life, besides heredity, are diet, exercise, creative pursuits and frequent, pleasurable social interactions. The entire lifestyle at Woodland Pond is geared to foster these factors in ways large and small; perhaps that's why I'm surrounded with smiling, lively and interesting people each time I leave my apartment and venture forth into the community. Every day brings new discoveries and stimulating interactions. Yet, as a writer and an avid reader, what I also appreciate is the privacy I enjoy in my own spacious apartment for those hours that I devote daily to private pursuits. In offering me equally attractive public and private spaces, Woodland Pond affords me the best of both possible worlds.

I wanted to come here while I was still healthy and spry and eager for new experiences so that, relieved of all the burdens of owning and maintaining a home, I could devote my time fully to my writing and the many activities that the

Woodland Pond community offered, while supported by a fellowship of vital, caring people.

I honestly feel compelled to interrupt my fiction writing and to record this brief personal history of my life at Woodland Pond as a means of expressing my gratitude to the entire professional staff who contribute immeasurably to the joyful ease of my daily living, and to my fellow residents who welcome all new entrants with warm solicitude. As one resident stated shortly after my arrival, "We're your new family." These words proved to be prophetic as Woodland Pond quickly became not just my current address but my cherished home.

Let me stress that this is my **personal** history of experiencing Woodland Pond. Other residents, of course, might have different views, but I respectfully claim the right to share my personal story which has been totally positive from day one. No community of our size and complexity has achieved perfection in every aspect of its functioning. However, I'm continually impressed by how any small concern I have ever shared with the administration has been expeditiously addressed and followed up. I will state at the outset that I have always made a conscious effort to focus on everything that's positive in my life and to see the glass as half full rather than half empty, but I certainly have encountered people who seem to embrace the opposite view.

For anyone considering moving to Woodland Pond, I offer my own experience as a possible insider's guide. Perhaps, as I did, you want a change, are ready for new adventures while still living independently but enjoying the security of available healthcare resources you may need in the future. If you want to continue to grow, to be nurtured by new and lasting friendships and to pursue your interests among stimulating people and beautiful surroundings, then Woodland Pond is the place for you. Come join our happy, dynamic community. I'll look forward to greeting you.

Taking Stock

The occasion of my seventieth birthday was a milestone causing me to honestly assess my current life and think hard about my future. I enjoyed good health and financial security but was living alone and no longer had a family. My current home was a place I cherished: a sprawling seven-room condominium on the North Shore of Long Island perched high atop a one-hundred-eighty-foot bluff with a panoramic view of the Long Island Sound and the undulating shore of Connecticut. Every Fourth of July I invited friends to join me on my terrace and enjoy a kaleidoscope of fireworks exploding across the many towns dotting the Connecticut shoreline.

A sandy beach lay directly below me at the bottom of a private stairway. Across the parking area in the rear of my building was an Olympic-size pool and four tennis courts, adjacent to a private golf course whose gourmet restaurant was a five-minute walk from my door.

My apartment's vaulted ceilings and multiple skylights created rooms suffused with light that reflected off the bleached oak floors. With all the public rooms directly facing the water, strategically placed mirrored panels captured and multiplied the panoramic views, while warm paint colors and a large fireplace created a cozy feeling at night.

Over the course of my seven-year occupancy, with the outlook that this would be my permanent home in retirement, I had spared no expense in adding all the bells and whistles that home magazines touted as the latest trends: granite counters, stainless steel appliances, a large jet-air soaking tub and a separate ten-jet shower. Hand-painted murals, crown moldings and custom window treatments further enhanced my living environment.

In surveying my residence I realized that, yes, I had invested time, energy and money in creating a home that was modern, comfortable, spacious and cheerful, with awe-inspiring views and no burdens involving exterior maintenance. This all seemed like the perfect environment for my writing endeavors in my retirement years; yet, something was missing. There was no real sense of community, no true sense of neighborliness, no supportive warmth. The cold nor'easter winds that frequently swept across the Long Island Sound and buffeted the high bluffs of my condo complex seemed to have seeped into the hearts of many residents, rendering them indifferent to their neighbors.

Although I had been a resident for seven years and had served on the Board of Managers for four years, thereby affording me wide exchanges with fellow residents and a broad perspective on our entire community, I had to candidly admit that this was a pervasively impersonal environment in which to live. Naturally, there were exceptions, for I had developed new, treasured friendships with a few other residents (who also candidly commented on the cold community atmosphere) but, still, the general climate was not a friendly one. On further reflection I concluded that this could be attributed to several factors.

My condo complex, with over one –hundred units, was nearly evenly divided between full-time and part-time residents. Some of the part-time residents—many from Manhattan—used their apartments throughout the year on most weekends while others occupied their units only during the summer or vacation time. Some owners—maybe ten percent—had purchased their units as investments rather than homes and were usually clamoring for relaxation of the stringent rental regulations the Board had established.

While the complex had been built in the 1980s and marketed as "luxury condominiums," a dip in the real estate market a few years after its opening had attracted new buyers with limited assets who, while being full-time residents, opposed the "pioneer" owners' efforts to continually enhance our community's attractiveness and amenities.

This difference in attitude caused a rift that sometimes divided the residents into openly hostile camps.

There was still another subset among the full-time residents comprised of older couples who had chosen to leave large homes in wealthy Long Island enclaves to move to our community. Upon seeing the broad spectrum of socio-economic backgrounds within our complex, they assumed a lofty, distant air and would only impart a terse, supercilious greeting when encountering neighbors, while pursuing their social contacts elsewhere.

Finally, and perhaps most importantly in my frank analysis, there was the issue of age. Our owners spanned the gamut from mid-thirties to late seventies, with every age group—young, middle and older—seeming to prefer associating with neighbors of similar age. For someone like me, born in Manhattan and having experienced a peripatetic life as a child of a career naval officer while growing up in seven different states, such limited social interactions were unacceptable.

When you've lived in cities, suburbs and the country, you develop a fondness for diversity of all sorts.

So here I was at seventy, divorced after many years of marriage and living alone, surrounded by too many people who, for multiplicities of reasons, were either disinclined to be friendly or were downright unfriendly to the point of blatant rudeness; hence, my conclusion that this was a frosty, indifferent environment for me to be thinking about spending the remainder of my years. I had a moment of stark epiphany when I asked myself this question: If I ever had a health emergency at 2 a.m., whom would I feel comfortable in calling for help?

My immediate answer saddened and alarmed me. My one neighbor of whom I was very fond was severely crippled with arthritis and could offer no assistance. Another neighbor who had become a close friend had remarried and moved away. My other close friends were at least an hour away. The blazing reality was that there was no one. From that moment on, my vulnerability was uppermost in my thoughts and my entire perspective on my present living conditions changed. I began to think of different arrangements that could meet all my needs for comfort, security and community, both now and in the future.

Exploring the Unknown

In the next two years I explored the internet for various types of retirement communities and ultimately rejected the concept of separate houses behind locked gates and condo complexes with age restrictions. My challenge, as I defined it more sharply, was to find some community that allowed me a full and independent life style while I was vigorously active, but could also accommodate my future needs if I lived a long life and eventually required either some daily assistance or full nursing care. The prospect of making several more moves—say, from my next home to unknown places for advanced care—was discouragingly daunting. I was eager to avoid so much uncertainty in future, more vulnerable years.

I had also considered the possibility of hiring health aides in the future if I needed them and was still living independently. A doctor friend, based on first-hand experience with his patients, enumerated the pitfalls and perils of this practice which quickly persuaded me to abandon this notion as a future viable option.

It was during this preliminary exploration that I first learned of the CCRC (Continuing Care Retirement Community) approach: a community that you entered as an independent resident, occupying an apartment or cottage of your choice, and then, should future needs require more care, transferring to one of several units—Assisted Living, Memory Care, Skilled Nursing—all within the same complex. The CCRC approach guaranteed that I would be taken care of in my advancing years, thereby alleviating my concerns about an unknown, uncharted future.

Given my circumstances, a CCRC made perfect sense as the right placement for me, but I still had many questions to be answered. I contacted an established CCRC in my area, read all the information sent to me and, encouraged by everything I learned, made an appointment for an initial visit.

I can vividly recall the mounting excitement I felt as I met a sales representative and we toured several attractive apartments of varying sizes and some spacious cottages, all set on expansive acres of rolling grassland, woods and streams, ending at the edge of the Long Island Sound. Next we toured the public spaces: indoor swimming pool, community meeting room, pub, several dining areas for formal and informal dining and the library/computer room. We quickly traversed several other spaces that began to blend together in forming my positive impression of many diverse activities being offered within the community under one roof.

During my three-hour tour, with another hour spent at lunch where I saw the extensive menu offerings for both lunch and dinner, my sales representative made special efforts to introduce me to many residents with whom I briefly chatted. They all raved about their current lives in this community and how relieved they were not to carry the burden of home ownership anymore.

When I asked one resident why she liked living in this community, she smiled and spoke enthusiastically: "This is like living in a luxurious resort where we have wonderful amenities, enjoy delicious meals served in elegant surroundings, and all our needs are taken care of by a solicitous staff." This lady was an artist and she stated that now she had more time to devote to her painting. Since I always tried to carve out several hours each day for my writing, I duly noted this advantage.

From all my brief chats with residents and my observations of others in the various areas I visited, a general impression was forming that led me to the realization of a most important consideration in joining any Continuing Care Retirement Community: a congenial, comfortable and compatible social environment.

A stilted, artificial style of speaking and a grand manner seemed to pervade most of the conversations I had on this visit. This reminded me too much of some of my current neighbors with their *nouveau riche* airs—a complete turn-off. Several residents' immediate references to their former big houses in the Hamptons or their summer homes on the Cape seemed to be inserted in our brief exchanges solely to impress me. At lunch I noted the elegant attire of the ladies and was informed that jackets for men were required for dinner.

When I retired as a school district administrator, university lecturer and curriculum consultant, I gave away most of my suits and a great many ties, for these articles were part of my professional attire. In my private life I was strictly casual if not downright sloppy. Retirement brought me the freedom of giving scant attention to how I was dressed, and the thought of returning to an environment of prescribed/proscribed attire was not attractive. I made a mental note to make a casual dress code a priority in all my future CCRC explorations.

Rather than a "luxurious resort," as the artist had described this community, I felt it more accurately resembled an exclusive country club, lacking any apparent diversity and filled with smug and competitive members—not something I'd be interested in joining.

The last half hour of my visit was spent with the Chief Financial Officer who reviewed the costs for apartments of various sizes and cottages of various locations—those closest to the Long Island Sound had the highest prices. The figures were impressively expensive and, in some cases, staggering, confirming my impression of an exclusive—and rich—country club. I left the premises having rejected this community as the one for me, but more confirmed in my feeling that a CCRC was the right move to make. I just had to find the right one.

I next contacted another CCRC not far from where I lived and arranged a visit. This community I rated much more favorably with its friendly, easy-going and unassuming residents, its listing of numerous activities and a palpable *joie de vivre*. The price for a two-bedroom, two-bath apartment was reasonably within my means and the layout, including a gas fireplace and a small porch, was attractive. However, there were some negatives.

Of all the common spaces available to residents in any CCRC, two were of primary importance to me: the swimming pool and the library. Swimming laps had been my favorite exercise throughout my adult life. More importantly, it was the only form of exercise that I would do consistently. Working out on treadmills and stationary bicycles was, to me, so tedious that I could find a dozen excuses for skipping it. A consistent walking regimen was conditional upon the weather and my mood. I enjoyed swimming and didn't have to push myself to swim a minimum of fifty laps each weekday. However, a pool had to be long enough to do laps comfortably and it should be placed in an attractive setting.

An appealing library was also important. With the many years occupied in pursuing my degrees and post-doctoral research, and then devoting my professional career to educational settings, I felt as if I had spent a major portion of my life in libraries and enjoyed their quiet atmosphere and invitation for learning. Now, as a writer and lover of books, I knew I would use any community's library as an alternate writing and reading venue when I grew restive in my apartment, and I wanted it to be a warm, inviting space.

At this CCRC I was disappointed with the swimming pool because a portion of one end was taken up by a long ramp to accommodate disabled swimmers in entering the water, thereby diminishing its length and inhibiting lap swimming. The library was a relatively small space tucked away in a mezzanine above the lobby, like an afterthought. With its low ceilings and small windows, it had a decidedly cramped feeling. I could picture medieval monks dutifully copying and illustrating sacred manuscripts but I couldn't picture myself enjoying this space.

Another negative was the long, narrow, windowless hallways leading to the apartments, creating a claustrophobic feeling. Finally, the few available apartments overlooked an interior courtyard. I hadn't expected to equal the extraordinary view of my condo but this vista was at the other extreme and further advanced my uneasy feelings of being closed in.

I was clearly on a learning curve and, based on this visit, I made another mental note to establish a decent view providing both privacy and reasonably attractive focal points as a priority for any apartment I inspected in the future.

Fate now intervened in closing my mind completely to this community. The complex abutted a heavily trafficked six-lane highway, rendered invisible (except for the noise) by an artificially placed copse of trees. As I left the community and pulled out into the center lane of this major thoroughfare, a young man driving fast in the left lane suddenly swerved directly in front of me, causing me to slam on my brakes, narrowly avoiding a collision. He then lurched into the right lane, causing another driver to come to a screeching stop while the man's car raced to the corner and made a right turn.

Long Island is known for its ever-burgeoning population and the resulting pattern of consistently heavy traffic, impatient drivers and impulsive moves—conditions which, based on my own experience, extended to the very easternmost tips of the island. This was not the first time I had encountered dangerous drivers threatening my safety, but as I sat in my car, momentarily stunned, my thoughts raced ahead to the future when I would be older. If I was still capable of driving, did I really want to be driving in these challenging conditions? Of course, my instant answer was NO, and I made an immediate decision to find a CCRC in another area.

Eureka!

At the time of my preliminary exploration of CCRCs, there were only twelve of them licensed in New York State, several of which were located in western New York and these I eliminated. My internet search showed several in the lower part of eastern New York, but only Woodland Pond at New Paltz was in the mid-Hudson Valley area, which intrigued me.

Years ago I had spent a weekend at Mohonk Mountain House with its magnificent grounds and majestic views, just outside the village of New Paltz, leaving me with a fleeting but positive impression of the surrounding area. I liked the idea of a large university with all its cultural and intellectual offerings situated in the town, and the casual and stimulating atmosphere that college students and faculty always added to any setting.

On my first visit to Woodland Pond, everything I saw and heard impressed me favorably, including the convenience of being only three minutes away from the New York Thruway which, despite its proximity, didn't intrude on the pastoral serenity of the community. As my special friend Katy and I walked around the premises with a marketing representative, every person we encountered in passing offered a friendly greeting and warm smiles. All the activity rooms were filled with lively, animated residents doing art or woodwork projects, playing cards, participating in various classes, working on committees or exercising in the pool or the workout room.

We especially took note of all the paintings, drawings, photographs, sculptures and handicrafts done by residents that adorned the public spaces—an impressive testament to the full range of artistic talents in the community. I happily noted that the heated indoor swimming pool, located in a splendid setting with a wood cathedral ceiling and multiple windows outlining pleasant vistas, was a generous size for lap swimming. Sensibly, a hoisting device had been installed on the deck at the shallow end of the pool to accommodate disabled residents, rather than a long ramp jutting into the water and reducing the swimming area. A large, inviting hot tub sat next to the pool.

The pub area, with its dark wood, curved bar, art-deco fixtures and etched glass, looked inviting, and the dining room and adjacent bistro area were also very attractive. I was relieved to learn that jackets were not required at dinner and that dress was strictly casual. But our tour guide had saved the best for last.

The library was, by far, the most beautiful, well stocked and spacious library of any CCRC I had visited. At the center of this generous space, naturally illuminated with light pouring in from many windows, was a wall-high rock fireplace surrounded by comfortable wing chairs. I could envision myself ensconced in one of them, reading, or writing at one of the long tables situated around the room. I took note of the several computers with free internet service and the free photocopy machine for residents' use.

We visited several cottages and apartments of different sizes, all with attractive details, but one apartment stood out and I immediately coveted it: a two-bedroom, two-bath end unit with extra windows and a direct view of Skytop Tower on Shawangunk Ridge and, off to the right, the Catskill Mountains. This panoramic vista would be a great substitute for the one I currently enjoyed, and I could picture myself living, writing and entertaining here with gusto, continually stimulated by the view.

Speaking of views, one of the most impressive features of Woodland Pond, for me, was its magnificent surroundings: eighty-three acres owned by Woodland Pond including hiking trails and natural ponds, and beyond the property, huge forested preserves with the mountains sharply silhouetted in the distance. Nature's full and abundant beauty surrounded me wherever I looked. All these inspiring long-view and near vistas greatly enhanced the attractiveness of the interior public areas as well as the individual residences from which they could be seen.

The marketing representative had arranged for Katy and me to have lunch with Craig Haight, a resident Marketing Ambassador, and his wife Betsy. I look back on that day now and think how blessed I was to encounter these two wonderful people, to spend time with them and instantly succumb to their charm and wit and warmth. Over a tasty lunch Katy and I asked many questions, to which we were given full and honest answers. They invited us to their apartment and our lively conversations continued.

Before we parted I felt sufficiently relaxed with Craig and Betsy to ask my final, burning question. Was this a community where a political and social liberal like me would feel comfortable? Craig assured me that while there was a broad gamut of political and social views contributing to a dynamic environment, I would find many people of liberal persuasion. Days later, as a token of my appreciation, I sent Craig and Betsy an inscribed copy of one of my books in which my liberal biases against our current wars were most pronounced. Craig sent me a thank-you note, reassuring me that I would fit in nicely at Woodland Pond.

Katy and I finished our visit with a stroll around the grounds, admiring its fountains, waterfalls, plantings and benches. We sat for a while, silent and still, absorbing the scene and reflecting on our visit. As we drove away we were both filled with enthusiasm for this community. Katy, a life-long artist, art teacher and art department chairperson, had loved everything, with one exception: the carpeting in the lobby and public spaces. But then she said, "You can't reject a wonderful community because of carpeting," and I fully agreed.

As the days passed I kept picturing myself in that end unit I loved, and my enthusiasm for Woodland Pond only grew. I had also learned that if I ever had to move to Assisted Living, Memory Care or Nursing Care in the Health

Center, I would be in a private room. This guarantee of privacy was very important to me and not guaranteed by some other continuing care communities I had investigated. Still, I cautioned myself, this was a great leap of faith into unchartered territory and a major life-changing decision and should not be made capriciously or quickly. I arranged a second visit accompanied by a couple whom I considered family, and they came away with a ringing endorsement of Woodland Pond as a great place for me.

In the months that followed my second visit, I made two additional visits—more than a six-hour round-trip drive so I must have been serious. I also made numerous phone calls to Woodland Pond with many questions resulting from my reading all the informative material that had been given me. I found the entire staff, from marketing personnel to the concierge ladies (more about them later), to the administrative members, generous with their time and thorough in their answers, all rendered in a spirit of frankness and cordiality that further impressed me.

On one of my visits, I attended a presentation by current Woodland Pond residents and one speaker made a strong impression on me. Joan Kleinegris exuded enthusiasm in speaking about her very busy daily schedule of activities, her apartment and her new-found friends since joining the community. A happier, more contented and vibrant person I could not imagine!

There was one other CCRC to which I had given serious consideration and I made one more visit to that community. In meeting with the marketing director I told her frankly that my choice was between her community and Woodland Pond. She then made a comment that would affect me profoundly. She said, "Ultimately you'll decide on the place where your heart is." That night I lay in bed pondering her words and then I had my answer. My heart was already residing in Woodland Pond.

While so many hurdles remained, especially the sale of my condo and the chance that the one apartment I desired above all others would still be available, my mind was made up and my path of action clear.　Excitement and anxiousness interrupted my sleep that memorable night.

Woodland Pond, a non-profit organization, has a policy whereby ninety percent of the required entrance fee for incoming residents is placed in escrow and is returned to the resident or the resident's heirs upon leaving the community or passing away.　Other CCRCs I had visited had a similar policy, but they also offered another entrance arrangement that reduced the initial entrance fee.　Over a four-year period, a percentage of this entrance fee would be subtracted each month from the amount returned to the resident upon leaving the community.　At the end of four years of residency, no money would be returned.

Because of my unusual situation of no longer having any family and no immediate heirs, with my assets bequeathed to New York University and Columbia University (in gratitude for the scholarships and fellowships I had received from both institutions in the course of pursuing four degrees), I was looking for this diminishing-return policy at a reduced entrance fee. I expressed my wish to the administration and they immediately initiated the paperwork to submit to New York State for permission to add this policy to their admissions process. To my astonishment and delight, approval from the state was granted in an amazingly short time (for wading through bureaucratic ranks), thanks, I subsequently learned, to the tenacious follow-up of Michelle Gramoglia, Woodland Pond's Controller (modern spelling).

A term of one year, which could be extended, for the sale of my condo, was a reassuring condition of the Woodland Pond contract. I had consulted a lawyer specializing in elder law, and armed with a thorough knowledge of all the contract's provisions, I now negotiated some minor, individual details with Woodland Pond's Executive Director before signing the contract and making my deposit. With a clear understanding of the money I could save if, in the future, I had to spend extended time in the Health Center, I opted for the Life Care program for an additional up-front cost.

The die was cast and I was hurtling forward into the unknown, hopeful that I was making the right decision and that things would go smoothly with all the work that had to be accomplished before I became a resident of Woodland Pond.

The Big Move

There's an old real estate maxim that says,
"regardless of the current market conditions, any
property will sell if it's priced right." I applied
this guideline to my own home in setting a selling
price.

As a member of my complex's Board of
Managers I knew that eleven units were currently
on the market and no unit had sold in nearly two
years. The prices listed in real estate advertise-
ments for these units reflected their highest
valuations in 2007, before the real estate bubble
burst. Owners were unrealistically seeking those
highest prices in the slow, downturn market of
2011 and thus were unable to sell. I was
determined not to make the same mistake. I
wasn't looking to make a killing, for now that I

had committed my future to living in Woodland Pond, I was eager to see my resolve become a reality.

I had the largest unit in the complex, which had been previously owned, enlarged and customized by the man who sponsored the complex. My unit had the best views, not to mention all the upgrades I had made. I contacted a local real estate agent and told him I wanted to set a realistic price that would be irresistible to any prospective buyer. He came up with a figure and, to his astonishment, I reduced it by ten thousand dollars and signed an exclusive contract with him.

The agent warned me that even with the very attractive price I was asking, the market was so sluggish that it could be many months before a sale was made. I resigned myself to this eventuality while still hoping for the best. My condo was to be featured in his agency's advertisement the following Sunday and would be available for showing on Monday. After seeing that the unit was in top display mode, I went away for the weekend.

On Saturday, the day before its official listing, while in upstate New York with close friends—the same couple who had visited Woodland Pond with me and loved it—I received a call on my cell phone.

"Are you sitting down?" the agent asked. He then went on to tell me how he had received a call from another agent who said she had a couple who had looked at every listed unit in my complex but had found nothing to their liking. She asked my agent if he knew of any units about to be listed.

"The biggest and the best," was his reported response, and on Saturday morning the couple had come to view my unit and immediately offered the full asking price. Evidently I **had** made the price irresistible (and was still making a significant profit on the sale). My agent explained that the couple was offering the full price because they expected a bidding war once other people saw the unit. Furthermore, this was an **all-cash** deal. The real estate gods were clearly smiling on me.

I think I had been sitting down at the start of this conversation, but by this time I was standing and hopping about in mounting excitement, and my friends quickly joined me in a little impromptu jig of jubilation. I had clearly beaten the realty odds and instantly saw no further major obstacle to my taking up residence at Woodland Pond. Just a hell of a lot of work ahead!

I will admit that a momentary temptation crept upon me, rationalizing that if this couple was so eager to buy my unit, others might be equally eager and a bidding war could ensue. However, remembering the old adage about "a bird in the hand is worth two in the bush," I quickly quashed any hesitancy on my part. I accepted the offer and celebrated my good fortune with my friends for the rest of the day. But there was more good news to come.

The very next day my agent again contacted me and said the couple was now asking if I would be willing to sell them the furnishings and selected pieces of art. This offer was truly serendipitous because the dimensions of the rooms in my condo were different from the rooms in my Woodland Pond apartment, and I had already determined that I would have to sell most of my oversize furniture and buy pieces on a smaller scale. I readily agreed.

The following weekend I met the couple and we quickly came to a mutually agreeable price for all of my furnishings except my master bedroom set which, although large, would fit nicely in my spacious new master bedroom. I was also taking my library bookcases and many of my books, for I had already decided to convert the second bedroom of my new apartment into a den-library, since overnight guests to Woodland Pond could stay in the available guest suites.

Despite having disencumbered myself of so much furniture, I, like any senior, had collected during my adult life a host of things that were mostly packed away in my large attic storage room, as well as dishes, linens, various collectables and odds and ends that I was determined not to haul to my new abode. The rule I established was simple: If I hadn't used it or looked at it for over a year, I wasn't taking it with me just to stuff it in some closet or drawer and not use it for another year.

I contacted two of my favorite local charities that I had been supporting through the years and donated everything that did not meet my rule. They made five trips with a filled van and were very grateful. I was relieved and happy to see everything go, and for a good cause.

My one indulgence, I admit, was my large book collection, but even here I established a separate rule that I would only take books I had not yet read or the classic books I wanted to read again. As I surveyed the titles of over two thousand books and found so many that I had not yet read, the dramatic scope of my book addiction hit me. I simply could not resist buying books that appealed to me, whether found through book reviews in the Sunday *Times* and the *New Yorker*, spotted while browsing in book stores or heeding recommendations of friends.

As my stacks of "books to read" crept beyond my bookshelves and invaded nooks and crannies in every room of my home, I would rationalize my addiction by telling myself that I would get around to reading all of them in my later years when my physical activities might be limited. I was like a squirrel storing up nuts for the winter. Now I acknowledged that even if I lived to be at least one-hundred-twenty-five, and spent all those additional years in reading marathons, forgoing sleeping, eating and bathing, I could not possibly read them all. Draconian measures had to be taken and now was the appropriate time.

On one of my visits to Woodland Pond I learned that the impressive collection of books in the library had all been donated by residents—in itself a persuasive testament to the literary and educational level of this community—and I was delighted to continue that tradition by offering several hundred of my books to the library. To this very day I discover my books displayed in various public areas besides the library. I have also donated copies of six of the published books I had written. There is no doubt about it: we are a reading community.

I made one more trip to Woodland Pond to arrange for several changes and some additional amenities for my apartment. I found the administration and facilities staff, especially John Smith, to be extremely cooperative and very fair in their charges.

In less than three months I turned over the keys to my condo to the new owners. Their realty agent at the closing said she had never had a sale go so smoothly and felicitously, and we all hugged before departing. My severely pared-down possessions were packed into a small moving van. The new furniture I had ordered had been delivered directly to Woodland Pond and was already set up in my new home, thanks again to the very accommodating facilities staff.

I jumped into my car and eagerly headed for New Paltz and the next chapter of my life. At this point I was feeling some trepidation since everything had moved so quickly. Until I experienced day-to-day life in my new community I was leaping into the unknown. With mingled feelings of joyful anticipation and looming anxiousness I sped up the New York Thruway to my new home—possibly the last home I might have. I was going to an area that I was largely unfamiliar with and to a community where I knew no one except my brief, positive interactions with Betsy and Craig Haight.

I could not have known at that time that this move to Woodland Pond would prove to be one of the best decisions I had ever made, resulting in a level of contentment and joyfulness I could never have anticipated.

Transitioning

I vividly remember my first few days at Woodland Pond as a delightful and auspicious beginning to my residency. The changes and upgrades to my apartment had all been meticulously completed. A welcoming tote bag with a Woodland Pond logo, filled with essential household items, sat on my kitchen counter along with a cheery note from the marketing department. I had been informed that I had a secure storage cubicle in the basement and had arranged for my movers to deliver my Christmas decorations directly to the cubicle.

In the first few hours after my arrival, as I supervised the movers' arranging my bedroom set and bookcases, several of my new neighbors dropped by to welcome me, and I could not have wished for a friendlier introduction. Additionally, members of the resident Welcome Committee called and invited me to join a group at dinner.

That first evening, as I sat with five other residents, the conversation was lively, interrupted with much laughter of a self-mocking nature, for one of my first observations about my dinner companions was how readily they could laugh at all the challenges of being senior citizens. They seemed to take everything in stride and consciously maintain a positive attitude. My happy conclusion was that wisdom, along with years, had accrued from formative life lessons.

For several nights thereafter I received dinner invitations from other members of the Welcome Committee as well as several of my neighbors, so that I was never alone at dinner time. The open seating plan gives residents great variety in choosing dinner partners: you can make dates with friends and neighbors for lunch or dinner, or you can arrive at the hostess station and fill an empty space at a table. I found this arrangement an easy way to meet a lot of people.

At one of those introductory dinners a lady at my table said, "We'll bombard you with all the basic questions so we can quickly get to know you a little better and then we'll just enjoy your company." I, too, had many questions for them regarding myriad details about life at Woodland Pond, all of which they answered fully and patiently, thereby helping greatly in my settling in.

During the course of those first meals—and I should note how pleased I was with my food and the courteous and diligent young men and women who served us (but more on that subject later)—many residents, alerted to my arrival by a notice in the mail room which is the customary procedure, came to my table to introduce themselves and wish me a hearty welcome. Consequently, I was already feeling relaxed and at home.

Each evening when I returned to my apartment, I couldn't help but recognize a major difference in my new lifestyle. I was spending two very pleasant hours in an attractive dining room, enjoying a tasty and creatively presented multi-course dinner, surrounded with convivial company, rather than eating alone in front of the television, consuming some packaged food heated in a microwave. Life was definitely on the upswing!

I frequently asked my dinner companions what motivated them to come to Woodland Pond. Their reasons were many, although the well-appointed public and private spaces and the beautiful natural surroundings were a general lure, as well as release from the burdens of home ownership and all the attendant responsibilities. Their more specific answers varied: as parents with grown children, they wanted to continue living independently and not be a burden on their children as the aging process took its toll; their familiarity with the area and a desire to stay close to where they had lived and made friends; their greater proximity to family members, especially grandchildren; their easy access to splendid cultural offerings in the mid-Hudson Valley and, of course, New York City. Whatever the reasons, they all expressed great satisfaction with their choice—a harbinger, I hoped, of my feelings in the future.

The Welcome Committee, composed entirely of volunteer residents, also arranged a festive gathering for all the recent arrivals to Woodland Pond so that we could meet one another and ask any questions of the "veterans." This was a friendly and lively meeting that I found very useful.

I spent the first several weeks orienting myself to what I soon realized was a very busy and multi-faceted community and "learning the ropes." There was a lot to learn. Familiarizing myself with the hours for breakfast, lunch and dinner and Sunday brunch and the days and hours of the Market Basket—a store managed and operated exclusively by volunteer residents—was a first priority. Learning when the pub was open and how I could use my meal funds for wine or beer during these times was also a priority, given the markedly convivial profile of my fellow residents.

I learned that the Ulster Federal Credit Union had an on-site branch at Woodland Pond and also offered an ATM machine available at all times. The hairdresser in the on-site hair salon also cut men's hair—not that I had that much left. I familiarized myself with the monthly meal allowance plan, affording residents many options in managing their meals. I visited the Market Basket, conveniently located next to the lobby, and bought a few essential items like toothpaste and laundry detergent, and a few non-essential items like ice cream and crackers. To offset the ice cream and crackers, I began doing daily laps in the beautiful pool and even used the treadmill in the exercise room once in a while.

With my own mailbox in the postal room and my own cubby for internal communications either from the administration or from fellow residents, daily mail was easily picked up. I could even order stamps by filling out a form and they would be delivered to the concierge desk the next day.

Using the Resident Directory I began calling neighbors with whom I had not yet spent time and, in keeping with the informal custom of the community, inviting them to join me for dinner. No one ever refused my invitation and frequently the neighbors would invite me to come by for a drink before going to dinner. In this way friendly bonds were quickly established and it was fun to see how each apartment or cottage had been personalized and enhanced with decorations, family pictures and life mementos.

While I was now living independently in my spacious and comfortable apartment (with an awe-inspiring view), I recognized that Woodland Pond offered me a support system that unobtrusively monitored my well-being. I had emergency cords in my two bathrooms and a PERS (Personal Emergency Response System) button to wear around my neck while on the premises. If I was any place within the complex or strolling outside on the grounds and encountered any problem requiring immediate assistance, I only had to press the button to summon help. These devices afforded me a comforting feeling of security.

If you were not seen by the staff during the course of any day, you'd get a courtesy call in the evening. On those rare days when I was in the throes of creative writing binges and had hunkered down without leaving my apartment, I was always grateful for those thoughtful inquiries in the evening. The staff was definitely looking out for you.

All visitors and vendors must sign in at the concierge desk, and security personnel are on duty at night. While the doors of our main entrance are open during the day, no one gets by the vigilant eyes of our marvelous concierge ladies without being courteously challenged, and all secondary entrances are accessible only with an electronic identify card. Residents are asked to wear their identify card in all public spaces, and I found this practice very helpful in placing names with faces.

As a reformed smoker in my youth—and there is no one more rabidly anti-smoking than a reformed smoker—I was happy to note that Woodland Pond is a smoke-free environment not just within the buildings but extending to all the property. A mere whiff of smoke I now find repugnant, and it's hard to imagine how greedily I inhaled that smoke as a pleasurable habit, back in the era when every star in the movies smoked and smoking was a rite of passage for every teenage boy.

I can remember being in the Navy at boot camp when I was seventeen, and whenever our company commander would say "the smoking lamp is lit"—a figurative expression permitting us to smoke—all the young men would eagerly rush to the front of our barrack and, along with me, light up. Fortunately, recognizing the deleterious effects this was having on my body, I was able to kick the habit while still in my twenties. Now, I demanded and relished a smoke-free environment.

The full-time Wellness Nurse visited me and took a brief health history along with listing any medications I used. This information was placed in an adhesive pocket attached to the inside of a specific cabinet in my kitchen as a handy and important reference in the event of any health emergency. This placement of each resident's general health profile was regulated throughout the community.

I learned that Dedrick's, a local pharmacy, made free deliveries to Woodland Pond each weekday. You could establish a credit card account with them, phone in your order for medications, prescription or non-prescription, in the morning and, presto, they were at the concierge desk in the afternoon.

I also had a personal visit from the Director of Facilities who acquainted me with how any repairs to my apartment were done by the maintenance staff, including changing overhead light bulbs (they didn't want us on ladders), and explaining the simple work-order procedure. A visit from the Director of Dining Facilities focused on any special dietary restrictions I might have and how those needs could readily be met in the dining room. I could not have wished for more personal and helpful interactions with the administration.

I had long subscribed to the New York Times and now discovered that this newspaper and several local papers were delivered daily to the concierge desk. Packages that were heavy were delivered to my apartment. When the first snow storm arrived, I looked out my windows in the morning to see that the parking area had been plowed and all the cars had been cleared of snow. We even had a notary public on staff. All these discoveries added another layer of comfort and convenience.

If, on any day, I chose not to eat in the dining room, I could call and order lunch or dinner and pick it up at the hostess desk. If I were ill for a few days, I could have my meals delivered to my apartment. There was a private dining room that, for a modest fee, I could reserve for any personal gathering I wished to host, and for an additional modest fee I could have the private party catered by our excellent wait staff.

A strict rule against tipping any staff member was uniformly enforced, but the residents had established an Employee Appreciation Fund. We could show our thanks for all the services rendered us during the calendar year by making a personal donation to this fund, which was then distributed among the staff—not the administration—in time for the holidays. Thus our daily lives were freed from constantly deciding what and whom to tip; yet the appreciation and generosity of the residents were reflected in the total, impressive amount collected toward the end of the year and apportioned among our hard-working staff.

We also had an Applauds form which residents could use to identify individual staff members who had given singular service at some given moment, and that person received a five-dollar gift card and was identified in our monthly newsletter. My personal problem with this form was that I found all the staff, with rare exceptions, to be exemplary in their service and I could spend a portion of each evening identifying them while still forgetting to include some member. I quickly became spoiled, expecting and receiving excellent service.

I learned that it was important to put your unit number on your change-of-address form;

otherwise, the mail was delivered to the concierge desk where you might forget to ask for it, as I did frequently in those early weeks of residency.

I met with Dr. Arthur DiNapoli, the resident physician in the Health Center, encompassing our Assisted Living, Memory Care and Skilled Nursing units (and rehabilitation services). Dr. DiNapoli also took patients living independently and he became my general physician. Later I became a patient of a family of dentists who had set up a fully equipped dental office at Woodland Pond. Now, to see either my doctor or my dentist, all I had to do was walk to another part of the main building, without ever going outside. Free minor eyeglass repairs, free blood pressure checks and body massages for a reasonable fee were also offered on the premises. I felt totally pampered.

In any minor health emergency when Dr. DiNapoli was not on campus, I learned that there was a First Care health clinic less than ten minutes away. (I subsequently had occasion to use it and found it to be clean, efficient and well-staffed.)

I quickly discovered that "Control Central" at Woodland Pond is the concierge desk. The four ladies manning that desk in day and evening shifts--Lisa Cea and LaVerne Boos during the day and Marilyn Knoerzer and Lyn Murray at night and on weekends—are the very heart of Woodland Pond and simply the best public representatives our community could possibly have, with their gracious style, unending smiles, knowledge of all things pertaining to our complex and inexhaustible patience with all questions and requests.

No problem of mine was too small or too big that they didn't expertly handle with cheery dispatch and quiet efficiency, guiding me to the right person or supplying an immediate solution. They were of inestimable value to me in adapting to Woodland Pond, and to this day they contribute immeasurably to the smooth functioning of my daily life and, I believe, to the entire operation of our community. They set such a positive tone for Woodland Pond and we are fortunate to have them.

In private conversations with all four ladies, I heard how they all enjoy their jobs, working with the residents and the public, and their pride in their work is amply displayed in everything they do. Despite their hectic work conditions at times, with phones ringing and residents lined up in front of the concierge desk with questions, requests or concerns, nothing ruffles their equanimity or displaces their smiles. Because they're happy in their work, they make us feel happy in their presence. It's always a joy to interact with them and they all have a great sense of humor, as indicated by their lively response to my corny jokes.

Meeting with so many people in such a brief span of time, I found it challenging to put names with faces. The identity cards that residents wear were a great help, but depending on the distance between the person I was encountering and myself, my eyes could not always discern the name on the card. Fortunately, scattered throughout the building were albums containing pictures of residents with short biographical sketches accompanying each photo. I frequently consulted these albums as a useful aid to placing names with faces and getting to know a little bit about a lot of people.

I can never forget how my neighbor, Jean MacAvery, knowing I was new to the New Paltz area, offered me so much helpful information on local restaurants, the best farmers' produce stands and local points of interest, or how Halema Hassan, another neighbor, was so generous in recommending local health specialists and the location of the best cleaners, clothing stores, bakery, etc. Thoughtful gestures from the start were made by Bill Harris and his partner of forty-three years, Ed Steele. To be surrounded by such welcoming neighbors was most gratifying.

Woodland Pond published an updated internal phone directory each month along with an excellent monthly newsletter called *Woodland Life*. This multi-page newsletter features articles on upcoming events, recent community activities and celebrations, staff members who have received kudos from residents for exceptional service, residents' birthdays for the coming month and individual profiles of residents, accompanied with pictures, all underscoring the strong community spirit.

Having been responsible for publishing monthly newsletters and district-wide bulletins during the course of my school-district administrative career, I was singularly impressed with the quality of these newsletters, including their organization, excellent writing, attractive graphics and inviting tone. I made it a point to express my admiration to Gretchen Daum, Woodland Pond's Activities Coordinator and the designer of this publication.

More frequent written communications on an "as needed" basis are distributed to the community through "Chanticleer—The Information and News Voice of Woodland Pond."

I met Diane Boomhower, the lady assigned to clean my apartment, and she explained that I could also avail myself of having my bed linens changed every week, but I declined, preferring to undertake that task myself. However, for those people with any back problems, I could see how this service would be welcomed. I found Diane's cheerful, cooperative attitude—and thoroughness in whipping my apartment into shape with quick dispatch—to be another happy note in my unfolding song of praise for my new home.

My ongoing interactions with the members of Woodland Pond's maintenance crew could not have been more pleasant. Knowledgeable and helpful, they approach every task with professional dispatch and good spirits. As just one example, Steve Berry, no matter whether he's changing a light bulb, installing a shelf, delivering a heavy package or arranging tables for a committee meeting, always greets you with a broad smile. I feel that the collective eagerness of these competent men to be of service to the residents further enhances our comfort level.

I quickly realized that Woodland Pond could not be more conveniently located. In addition to our proximity to the New York Thruway, there was the reassuring discovery that the New Paltz

Emergency Squad and a fire house were both within a tenth of a mile from our front entrance.

Other conveniences became apparent. In less than five minutes I could be at the New Paltz Plaza Mall which houses, in addition to a Stop N Shop, a diner, a multiplex movie theater, a clothing store, sportswear store, dollar store, jewelry store, cleaners, bagel shop, Radio Shack, art gallery, flower shop and restaurants featuring Italian, Chinese and Jamaican food. For the ladies there is also a nail salon.

Directly across the street from the Stop N Shop is a Shop Rite, an Ace Hardware store and Dunkin' Donuts. For those who can't get enough of sweets, there's also a Freihofer's Bakery outlet just two minutes away.

In my previous home on Long Island, I had to travel many miles to encompass all of these conveniences that were now all within easy reach, only minutes away. How lucky could I get!

I was also grateful for the monthly Woodland Pond calendar that listed all the activities and events for each day. I placed it on the side of my refrigerator and circled the many things I might like to explore once I settled in. Clearly, there were offerings from morning to night of such an attractive variety that it seemed impossible for any person not to find something to his or her liking. In my case, a number of listed activities caught my immediate interest. I now eagerly looked forward to an active participatory life in my new community while still adhering to my daily allotted time for writing.

The Rhythm of Daily Life

I like to swim very early in the morning, and the challenge was to find a swim buddy—a community safety rule—who also enjoyed doing laps while the first rays of dawn filtered through the many windows of the natatorium.

I was lucky to find Marilyn Dilascio, a fellow resident originally from Canada where, at sixteen, she became famous as Marilyn Bell, her maiden name, for being the first person to successfully swim across Lake Ontario (a distance of some thirty-two miles), in twenty-one hours. This amazing accomplishment captured national newspaper headlines and earned her a Canadian ticker-tape parade with hundreds of thousands of cheering Canadians lining the route. Later she successfully swam across the English Channel and the Juan de Fuca Strait.

At nineteen, an age when life is just getting started for most people, Marilyn retired from competitive swimming events, married, raised four children and became a teacher. Her heroic swimming feats were made into a gripping full-length movie in 2001, titled *Heart: The Marilyn Bell Story*. She is honored in Canada as one of the country's ten top athletes of the twentieth century.

Marilyn, too, enjoys swimming at the crack of dawn, and we meet each weekday at 5:45 AM and swim laps for fifty minutes. I refuse to be intimidated by Marilyn's expert strokes and just paddle along on my side of the pool as she rockets back and forth on her side. We both agree that whenever the temptation arises to shut off the alarm clock, turn over and go back to sleep, the responsibility we feel to the other person is always a great motivation to rise and shine and swim.

After this workout, showers are available at the pool. Then I'll sometimes grab a muffin or fruit cup and coffee from the continental breakfast in the Pub and gab with the "breakfast group." Other times I'll return to my apartment, make a light breakfast and check the day's organized activities on my monthly calendar.

There are so many offerings each day that I find it necessary at the beginning of the month to highlight those that I want to attend or participate in, as a quick daily reference. While the dinner menu for the day is displayed outside the dining room early each morning, if I'm feeling lazy, I can also dial an internal number and listen to a recording of the menu offerings as well as the day's scheduled activities—a great convenience for residents with poor eyesight.

I'm usually at my desk by 8:30 for my morning minimum-three-hour writing regimen. During this dedicated time I have to guard against being distracted by the glorious vistas directly in my sight line from my desk: Skytop, Mohonk Preserve, the Catskill Mountains—Nature's resplendent beauty unfolding beguilingly as far as the eye can see, and a great temptation for idle ruminations. On the few days when I might wish to attend some morning activity, I have the time flexibility to be able to switch my writing schedule to the early afternoon.

Shortly after noontime I sometimes break for lunch at the Bistro. A regular menu of hot and cold sandwiches along with an assortment of side dishes is augmented each day with special dishes prepared by the chef. Salads are always available.

Depending on the day of the week, I have various regularly scheduled afternoon activities. On Monday it's the Pondaliers, a choral group composed entirely of residents led by our intrepid and patient fellow resident, Marion Thompson, a retired music teacher and choral director. She challenges us to stretch our vocal harmonizing and we proudly perform two concerts each year, always to a packed and enthusiastic audience. It's hard to decide who enjoys these concerts more: the audience or the performers.

On Wednesday I participate in the Play Readers Group. We usually number at least fifteen residents and enjoy reading plays aloud and discussing them. Moliere, Chekhov, Pinter, Lillian Hellman, A. R. Gurney, Becket and Shaw have been our more recent playwrights whose works we've read. Our group is led by Don Wildy, a retired SUNY New Paltz professor in the Communications Department (not a resident), a man of infectious enthusiasm and vast knowledge of the theater, with gifted insights in interpreting acclaimed plays. With his great sense of humor and boundless patience, he gently guides us to a greater understanding and appreciation through our reading and discussing these master works.

Each year Don adroitly directs (coaxes, cajoles, inspires) us in performing a public reading of some work for our community. It's at this time that his wide background in theater and his expertise as a director are clearly visible and most valued, as he patiently but firmly transforms us from mere readers into public performers. I was so inspired by Don's leadership and my fellow play readers' dedication that I interrupted my fiction writing to write a satirical play about a group of former movie stars living in a retirement home, all vying for attention and major roles in an upcoming benefit performance. I called it **Faded Glories** (or **When Egos Run Amuck**) and we had great fun presenting it to our ever-appreciative community.

On Thursday I join a dedicated group of charades players for much laughter as we silently act out quotations, common phrases or titles of books, plays, movies, songs and operas for our respective teams. On Friday I can again raise my voice in song along with other residents who join our dedicated Activities Director, Gretchen Daum, at the piano, for an hour of Simple Melodies. On Saturday morning I usually attend the regularly scheduled Men's Coffee, an hour of impromptu discussions and sharing of information. As an equal-opportunity community, we also have a Ladies Tea once a week but I'm not privy to what goes on there.

Saturday afternoon is my time for cards followed by a BYOB gathering. We're such a merry group that we also have informal happy hours during the week. Once a month there's a Happy Hour sponsored by the administration, with free wine and beer and tasty hors d'oeuvres.

Since I spend most of the winter season in Puerto Rico where Dominoes is a national pastime, I started a Dominoes group on Sunday evening that became quite popular and we usually have several games going.

While these activities might seem mundane, what imbues them with a special aura for me and, I believe, many others, is the zest and collective spirit that our coming together evokes. The specific activities become almost secondary to the good fellowship and high spirits we enjoy. I find them a welcome release from my concentrated writing periods of each weekday.

For the many residents who have no need to sequester themselves in the morning as I do, there is a challenging complement of scheduled activities throughout the day: strength class, water aerobics, water walking class, woodworking, drawing sessions, painting classes, dance movement, quilters, kneedlers (beautiful knitted afghans are donated each year to a veterans' hospital), spiritual discussion, meditation, political discussion, brainteasers, chi kung, ceramics class and several book clubs.

For those who enjoy cards and games, we have groups who regularly play Duplicate Bridge, Social Bridge, Canasta, Hearts, Mah Jongg (and the aforementioned Dominoes and Charades). Any resident is welcome to join.

Want to enhance your language skills? Join the groups that meet to practice Spanish, French and Yiddish. Additionally, any resident who has an interest in a particular subject or activity, such as I did with Dominoes, can place a notice on our community bulletin board and, voila, a new group can be launched. Calls for chess and poker players are among the latest postings.

We have a good number of residents who enjoy poetry of all kinds and we come together once a month to share poems we've selected, usually on one or two agreed-upon themes, but we're very informal and residents can choose poems that might be off-topic as well. Once a year we offer a poetry reading evening to our community in which we read a variety of dramatic, funny and even original poems for the residents' enjoyment.

In 2012 I offered an original satirical poem titled **Ballad of a Seventy-Five-Year-Old Man**

I am the very model of a modern septuagenarian;
I used to be carnivorous but now I'm vegetarian.
The doctor said to cut out meats because
they have cholesterol,
And then he said, avoid all sweets because
they're just bad overall,
And dairy products have much fat,
so limit butter to one pat,
And ice cream is a real no-no,
and now all candy has to go,
And cakes and pies and cookies too—
I'm left with chewing on my shoe,
"Cause vegetables go down so fast and
all they do is give me gas,
But still I really can't complain because
I'm feeling not much pain.

My dentist gave me gloomy news and
now I only sing the blues;
Fillings from so long ago are rotting and
they now must go,
And then he said, there's more to do;
your gums, once red, are turning blue.
I hear this news and heave a sigh because
his bill will be so high.
So now I've got a choice that's clear:
toothless or debts up to here!
My hearing's grown a little dim;
lip reading is my latest whim.
The hair that once lived on my head,
I started finding in my bed,
And then things really went 'awack'
as hair migrated to my back.
My eyebrows have no place to go,
so there they sit and grow and grow.
My list of doctors has grown long and
each one sings a different song;
My prostate's growing large alright,
so now I pee all through the night,
And pills and drops and ointments too,
I have to take more than a few.
Vacations are no longer fun,
I have to stay out of the sun;
Where once adventure I had sought, long naps are
now my favorite sport.
My bunions hurt, my back's a mess,

my eyes are growing dimmer.
I cannot tolerate much stress,
my bones are getting thinner.
So now you see what aging does,
it isn't very pretty,
But don't think that I tell you this because
I want your pity.
I still love life although at times
it can be pretty shitty.
I am the very model of a modern septuagenarian;
At times I can be cranky and
a full-fledged old contrarian.
But thanks to all my friends like you,
I somehow seem to muddle through,
And hope to share a lot more days and
make sure that each moment pays
With joy and fun and laughter too,
and many more things left to do,
So who cares 'bout those aches and pains when
love and zest for living reigns?
And warm hearts bolster one and all and
lift us up each time we fall.
That's how we rise above the din and
in the game of life we win!
So on and on the days will spin
'till I'm an octogenarian.

It's not Wordsworth or Shelly; it's merely humorous doggerel, but I certainly have fun when participating in this poetry group and our special evening of sharing our poems with the community.

Taking advantage of Woodland Pond's extensive natural surroundings, we have bird watching groups and walking/hiking groups in the spring, summer and fall. Afternoon activities are interspersed with monthly information meetings presented by the department directors. These are always lively and well-attended gatherings where residents voice concerns that are respectfully responded to by the various administrators in charge of Dining Services, Resident Services and Facilities, along with our Controller (spelled the modern way) and our Executive Director.

While I find these regularly scheduled meetings to be a frank and open forum for ongoing communication between residents and staff, I also find them tedious at times when any single resident or group perseverates on some topic. Usually, when this happens, some other resident diplomatically says "let's move on," and audible sighs of relief can be heard around the room. No one could ever accuse our community members of not being interested in every aspect of our community's proper functioning and willing to speak their minds. I respect and admire this dynamism but feel that it can be taken to extremes, to the detriment of the prevailing mood of optimism and good spirits.

The public meetings of the Resident Council are another vital link in the communication chain as well as another indication of the important role our residents play in contributing to the smooth and felicitous operation of our community. The Council is composed of nine members serving two-year terms, with a five-four alternate-year election sequence. The new members are elected annually by all the residents after a Nominating Committee (composed entirely of residents) has presented a bloc of candidates to the community at a Meet the Candidates meeting where each candidate gives a short speech in support of his/her candidacy.

The Resident Council meets regularly with the Executive Director and his/her administrative staff to discuss issues of importance to the general community. One member also attends the meetings of Woodland Pond's Board of Directors, serving as an additional communication conduit. The Council's open meetings with the entire community keep us informed of progress in specific areas or proposals for addressing residents' concerns.

As a new resident, what truly impressed me was the large number of committees that our residents have formed voluntarily to extend the scope and variety of our activities and amplify our voices in operating our community. These committees include but are not limited to: Activities, Art Studio, Décor Design, Gardening, Interfaith, Library, Market Basket, Operating Budget, Dining, Employee Appreciation, Political Affairs and the aforementioned Welcome Committee.

The Woodland Pond Foundation Committee plays an important role in enhancing our community life, but it took me a while to fully appreciate how it operates. All profits from our Market Basket store go to our Woodland Pond Foundation. Additional money is raised by individual donations, raffles, garage sales (of donated furniture, clothing and household items generously given by our residents), underwriting memorial plaques placed on benches around our campus, and other fund-raising activities. These funds can then be applied to supporting residents' requests for specific items or events that might have wide appeal to the community-at-large.

During my time at Woodland Pond I have always been impressed with the use to which the Foundation Committee has put its available funds, including: the excavation for, and purchase of, a flagpole and an American flag at the main entrance; book shelves and carousal racks and improved lighting for the library; shelving for a satellite library in the Health Center; a kiln for the art studio; an awning for the patio outside our Pub; and sponsoring the Kaleidoscope of the Arts

Show and Sale (of residents' original works—more on this event later).

All these committees are open to residents who wish to participate. In all my exploration of Continuing Care Retirement Communities in eastern New York, I didn't find one to rival Woodland Pond in the extent of self-actuated committees, activities and interest groups which, I believe, attests to the extraordinary vitality and diverse interests of our community members. During my first year I joined the Dining Committee, the Nominating Committee and the Activities Committee. In my second year I added the Décor Design Committee and Kaleidoscope Committee and agreed to chair the Nominating Committee. I found my work on these committees to be rewarding experiences reinforcing the impression of our residents' unswerving commitment to monitoring and improving all aspects of life at Woodland Pond.

During the spring, summer and fall seasons, those residents who enjoy gardening can secure their own plot within a designated area, and the variety of flowers, vegetables and plants grown by our gardening enthusiasts is continually a treat to behold. On my way from my apartment to the public rooms, I frequently stop to enjoy a wide view of the garden area, marveling at the "green thumbs" of my fellow residents and the creativity they apply in sculpting their plots. Unfortunately, I'm cursed with a "black thumb," since all my attempts at gardening resulted in catastrophe, so I'm doubly appreciative of these gifted gardeners.

Adjacent to our garden is a horseshoe pit where I occasionally like to test my pitching skills with friends. I can also improve my pool playing at the pool table in our Billiards Room, while simultaneously watching sports programs on a large flat screen television. Our Pub also offers a large flat screen television for public viewing, but whenever I'm in the pub I'm surrounded with lively people engaging in animated conversations, and I've never felt an inclination to watch television in such convivial gatherings.

If all these activities and interest groups aren't enough, we also have the SUNY New Paltz

Lifetime Learning Institute which frequently offers courses and lectures right here in Woodland Pond. For example, we began the New Year (2013) with a lecture by a retired publisher of twenty daily newspapers. His seductive topic was, "With So Many New Sources of News Today, What Can You Believe?" Throughout the months of January and February, a series of films featuring the music of Cole Porter was offered with expert commentary by the instructor. Residents have also enjoyed a series of memoir writing classes over the last three years. We even had a Driver Safety Course offered right here at Woodland Pond.

The town of New Paltz offers a great program called One Book, One New Paltz. Every year a book is selected and included in the university's curriculum and has a widespread readership throughout the town. Our many book-loving residents here at Woodland Pond—we have two book discussion groups running each month—also embrace this program Discussion meetings and other activities focusing on the book are held in various venues over a two-week period. I had the pleasure of moderating the lively discussion held at Woodland Pond last year for residents, university faculty and townspeople.

Under the title of Lifestyle Management, Marianne Turow, Woodland Pond's certified dietician, has recently been conducting a series of seminars pertaining to food and diet, which I and others have found very informative. Now if I only found vegetables to be as appetizing as pasta dishes, I'd be a successful dieter!

Given this plethora of offerings, it's easy to continue to be mentally stimulated, to explore new areas of interest and to grow, thanks to such a broad program that addresses the social, intellectual, spiritual and physical needs of all Woodland Pond residents. I've heard many residents comment that there aren't enough hours in the day to encompass all the activities they would like to join, but isn't this challenge a blessing in disguise? I certainly think so.

Here's a charming poem by one of Woodland Pond's merriest residents, Connie Hornbeck:

A HALLWAY TO MY HOME

A hallway to my home is really new to me
For driveway, lawns and sidewalks
is what I used to see
And my neighbors lived in houses, too,
seldom did we greet
But here in halls, a friend you'll find
in everyone you meet.
They're full of information 'bout
what goes on 'round the Pond
Like classes, dance, singing,
and the food, of which I'm fond.
Woodland Pond's an experience in living,
I'll agree,
But a hallway to my home,
is exactly right for me.

Connie captures the pervasive warmth of our community.

The Matter of Food

Dinner time is always a happy occasion for me and not just because I like to eat. I vary my dining pattern. Sometimes I'll call fellow residents and arrange to dine with them. Other times, I'll go to the hostess station and fill an empty place at a table, enjoying the variety of pleasant interactions this affords me.

Three times a week I eat with a group of seven ladies (or sometimes six ladies and one other man, my friend Len Kapner). When we're together our high spirits and laughter are so incessant that we usually are the most rambunctious group in the dining room, to the consternation, I'm sure, of a few, more sedate diners, but we enjoy one another's company so much that it's simply impossible to restrain our spirited fellowship.

And who can really resent any group of residents for obviously having such a good time, which is even supposed to aid digestion?

Here's a moment of candor, for I don't wish to suggest that Woodland Pond is some Shangri-La with no warts or challenges, although, for me, the good and joyful far outweigh the troublesome. Only once in all my informal placements at open tables did I ever experience a negative evening with two residents who spent the entire time complaining about everything—the weather, the food, the service, the cutlery, the stiffness of the napkins, their apartments, their health and the general condition of their lives. Any effort on my part to inject humor or light, positive topics was quickly rebuffed in favor of more grievances. For example, when I said the dessert was delicious, one resident said it was much too sweet and the other resident immediately said it was much too small.

I resolved that night never to sit with either of these two "grumps" again and consoled myself with the thought of how, in such a large community, I had only encountered two who were uncongenial dinner companions. Everyone else made a conscious effort to be good company and, naturally, I gravitated to those folks who were, to my mind, truly delightful. The open-seating policy contributed significantly to my happy state.

Here's a footnote to the incident I've just described. A few weeks later I saw a new lady resident being placed with these grumps and noticed that she seldom smiled throughout dinner. The next night I was placed at a table with her and another couple and found her to be a lively, jolly person with witty stories and a hearty laugh. At the end of our most convivial dinner, this lady said, "Thank you for such a positive evening." Pausing briefly, she added, "After my experience last night, I wasn't sure I had made the right decision." With a broad smile she said quietly, "I know now who to avoid in the future." Nodding my head, I answered, "I know exactly what you mean. We all learn that lesson early in our residency."

An immeasurable contribution to all my positive dining experiences is made by our wait staff. These young men and women, some still teenagers and most in either high school or college, are so pleasant, courteous and patient, especially with us seniors and our quirks, foibles and dietary restrictions, that many residents feel special bonds with them, and they are a delightful element in our daily lives. When I think back to my youth and candidly acknowledge my indifference to elderly people (probably anyone over fifty), having had no grandparents or senior relatives beyond the age of eleven, I find the warmth and solicitude of these young people remarkable—another gratifying dimension of daily life at Woodland Pond.

Now let's focus on the food, a basic interest of all residents or prospective residents in any community where meals are provided. In tackling this topic let me state frankly that I'm definitely into the basics—meat, seafood, pasta, vegetables and salads—but, as my portly profile reflects, I do like sauces, seasonings and assorted garnishes and especially desserts which, along with starches, I try to limit purely for health reasons.

My idea of food heaven would be a frequent diet of lobster bisque soup, crab cakes with dipping sauce, filet mignon with Béarnaise sauce and an occasional pepperoni-and-sausage pizza, followed with mint chocolate-chip ice cream or lemon meringue pie. Unfortunately, that heaven quickly becomes hell at two o'clock in the morning with acid indigestion, so I must eschew these adolescent delights—most of the time.

I mentioned previously that in the years since my divorce I had resorted mostly to packaged dishes heated in the microwave, but I also dined out at least once or twice a week and, having traveled extensively throughout the world, I've experienced both fine dining and exotic dishes. However, my palate was *never* refined to the point of requiring a constant assemblage of *haute cuisine.*

Having said all this as a preamble, I now must unequivocally state an independent view as **one** resident that I ALWAYS ENJOY THE FOOD!

Every night I marvel at the broad selection, with several soups and appetizers, at least two entrees plus a dinner-size salad of varying ingredients including steak, chicken and shrimp. There are assorted vegetables and starches, topped off with multiple desserts ranging from cakes and pies to assorted ice cream, fruit salad, whole fruit, and occasionally chocolate mousse and *crème brule.*

If nothing appeals to me from the dinner menu on any given evening, or if I don't feel like having a four or five-course dinner, I can select something lighter from the pub menu which offers four or five additional lighter items and more side dishes and vegetables. I can mix and match selections from either of these menus, multiplying my choices. Consequently, I can usually find something to my taste with complete satisfaction.

Yes, there are occasional misfirings—a dish not hot enough, some item undercooked, a tough piece of meat, not enough sauce or a mix-up in an order—and on those occasions, residents are encouraged to return the dish. Our Director of Dining Services, Jeff Hoffman, and our Dining

Room Supervisor, Ed Kelly, are dedicated to giving us a first-rate dining experience—I know because I serve on the Dining Committee—and, in my personal observations, they go to any length to make that goal a reality.

I suppose that in any community of seniors, food is the most talked-about and most commented-upon item, and Woodland Pond is no exception You'll get varying degrees of agreement or disagreement with my personal assessment, e.g., too much salt, not enough salt, etc. (along the lines of Goldilocks and the Three Bears—one bed too large, one bed too small). However, I also find that the ancillary aspects of my dining experience—table cloths, cutlery, glassware, the presentation of food on the plate— contribute appreciably to my pleasure each evening. At the request of our residents, the dinner and pub menus include information on both the sodium and caloric content of each item, a great help to those of us on restricted diets or trying to eat moderately.

Residents can order a half-portion and can take leftovers back to their apartment. Sometimes I'll just have two appetizers and a soup, or soup and a salad. The combinations are almost endless, depending on your palate, your creativity and your appetite that evening.

Wine of a reasonably good vintage for a very modest price is available by the glass or bottle, along with beer. I enjoy the wine offerings but oenophiles can, and do, bring their own. Residents who enjoy a cocktail with dinner can also bring their own.

Wednesday evening is buffet night and the many food choices usually center on some theme—Italian, Asian, Mexican, etc. Sunday brunch is a tantalizing assortment of breakfast dishes (made-to-order omelets, French toast, pancakes, eggs of your choice, fruit cup, salads, blintzes, assorted muffins, bagels and donuts).

If I eat moderately and take some time out to enjoy the company, I can then attack the lunch/dinner selections, with rotating items like sliced steak, roast beef, baked ham or

Chateaubriand, accompanied with vegetables and starches, a shellfish or fish selection, a quiche, pasta dish and several assorted desserts, all presented buffet-style. No dinner is served on Sunday, but the brunch is more than enough to sustain me throughout the day, with maybe some soup or a sandwich in my apartment at night. (Remember, all apartments have full kitchens.)

The far-ranging outside vistas from the dining room always enhance my dining experience, and I find the room itself, with its high ceiling, wall of windows and art-deco light fixtures, an appealing space. When the room is filled, the acoustic challenges can bother some diners, but the administration has taken steps to combat this ongoing issue, and more needs to be done.

This concludes my culinary dissertation with one further comment. Toward the end of a meal allowance cycle, it's always heartening to see how many residents have apportioned their monthly allowance to have funds left over, with which they buy food in the Market Basket store and donate these items to a local food pantry, reflecting our concern for others less fortunate than ourselves.

After dinner I can often attend additional evening events. Current popular movies are shown on Saturday and Sunday evenings (with matinee showings as well). One Friday evening of each month is devoted to showing a movie of some classical opera; another Friday evening is given to presenting a classic movie, spanning titles from the 1930s through the 50s, many of which the residents, like me, saw as children and enjoy seeing again. At the request of residents, on one Thursday of each month we now can also enjoy a foreign film. The community has a collection of DVDs that residents can borrow for private viewing in their apartments

Special events are frequently presented during weekday evenings after the dinner hours. The Political Affairs Committee arranges for candidates for local political office and aspiring school board members to address the community and engage in a question and answer forum, always a stimulating exchange, given the political savvy of so many of our residents.

Several authors and artists in our community, as well as their relatives and friends, have offered presentations on their books and paintings and photographs. I, too, had a Meet the Author evening in which I shared my writing process, my early development as a writer and my publishing experiences.

Convinced that the inspiring story of my swim buddy, Marilyn, should be shared with everyone, but knowing that she, being a very modest person, would never shine a spotlight on herself, I arranged a Meet the Champion evening in which we showed the full-length movie featuring Marilyn's heroic swim across Lake Ontario. Then she answered residents' questions, providing gripping details on what it's like to swim twenty-one hours, combating cold, fatigue, currents and moray eels.

Various children performances are scheduled in our Performing Arts Center (more about this later). The large turnout for all these presentations reflects the supportive, engaged nature of our community and our residents' zestful intellectual curiosity.

When I retire at night, after a good meal with congenial friends, frequently followed with some evening entertainment, I'm continually pleased with my day's events and looking forward to tomorrow. That's my definition of pure contentment.

The Spirit of Holidays

To really gauge the extraordinary spirit of our community, one has to see us on various holidays.

My first holiday experience as a resident was Veterans' Day in 2011. A formal afternoon program honoring the many residents who served in the armed forces was planned and, as a Navy veteran, I proudly participated. In our lobby Gretchen Daum, our tireless and dedicated Activities Coordinator, mounted a large picture display of many of our veterans in their youthful service days. My picture was from my graduation from boot camp at seventeen and I could hardly recognize myself—I was skinny and had hair! Assorted personal war memorabilia and souvenirs were also displayed.

The entire community packed our large Performing Arts Center for the formal ceremony. At one point the anthem for each service branch was played and the veterans of that branch stood to acknowledge the applause of grateful residents. I was seated next to a man who was having difficulty standing up when the Navy tune was played. I whispered that he didn't have to stand. He extended his hand to me and replied, "That's my anthem. Please help me." I pulled him up and we proudly stood shoulder to shoulder.

I'll digress briefly to share a noteworthy achievement within our community. So many of our residents are veterans that a community project was undertaken, led by residents Ray and Anne Smith and Pete Johnson, a former editor of the **New York Times**, to write up the war stories of our veterans as well as the memories of civilians during WW II and Korea. Since my years of service were after the Korean conflict, I did not participate. However, I edited one of the longer stories and found it fascinating.

At a celebratory gathering on the Fourth of July, 2013, the finished book titled ***Wartimes Remembered***: **World War II and Korea**, was unveiled—the exclusive product of Woodland Pond residents who contributed pictures, shared memories, recorded and edited stories and published the book.

In reading the stories of thirty-seven residents—some funny, some harrowing, some sad, but all engrossing and evocative of a dark historical period—I have never felt greater pride in living in this community with so many remarkable people. The appellation that Tom Brokaw gave to my fellow residents, The Greatest Generation, was illuminated by these compelling stories. I've given copies of this memorable book to friends to share with younger generations so that they may have a first-hand account of the courage and sense of duty exhibited by older folk when they were very young and caught up in world-shattering events.

Now back to our holiday spirit. In October we have a town-wide Oktoberfest at Woodland Pond with an "Oom-pah band," singing groups, craft booths, fall produce stall, dancing and many tasty dishes of German origin. Residents invite their children and grandchildren to attend and a good time is enjoyed by all.

Thanksgiving means the traditional turkey with all the trimmings. A festive mood pervades the dining room as residents are joined by family members to celebrate the holiday together. Ever mindful of those less fortunate than ourselves, we are especially generous in donating food to the local food pantry so that other families can have a good Thanksgiving dinner and celebrate this American holiday in the traditional manner.

This brings up an important point that I find refreshing. Family and friends of residents can visit Woodland Pond at any time. For those seniors who, like me, don't want to be isolated from younger generations, it's a constant pleasure to see young or middle-age parents with their children interacting with us seniors who dote on the kids.

We also interact with students from the New Paltz High School. The school has formed a partnership with Woodland Pond whereby, as part of a service learning class, students spend time with residents in Independent Living, Assisted Living and Memory Care on a number of fun and interesting projects.

Some projects call for students to gather information from seniors on their life experiences. Other projects allow for students to prepare special events for the residents, such as a *Cinco de Maya* party, or assist residents on projects involving the Library Committee. Through these various means, we interact with younger generations, and while we greatly enjoy these opportunities, we also hope that the students are gaining insights and knowledge from our life stories and the lessons they can impart.

Local high school students have also performed for us with scenes from musical plays they are presenting to the New Paltz community. Piano teachers have scheduled student recitals here at Woodland Pond. Thanks to all these activities, no one can say that we are isolated from youngsters, and we clearly relish their performances and their company.

We officially launch December's holiday season with a formal lighting of a huge Christmas tree set up in the main lobby and another ceremony honoring the lighting of the menorah on each of the eight days that tradition requires. Enthusiastic singing of appropriate songs and hymns accompanies these ceremonies, with residents of many faiths happily joining in.

Last Christmas we had another Christmas tree in our dining room festooned with red and green paper balls. Each ball had a written gift suggestion—the red for a local family's children and the green for a family victimized by Hurricane Sandy. The paper balls disappeared quickly from the tree as many residents were eager to participate in this charitable effort. In a moving ceremony, we presented our gifts to the local family, and the happiness exhibited by both the children and our seniors captured the essence of this giving season.

Our dining room also features a model train set, donated and set up by resident Bill Schnitzer. Upon seeing the trains each year, I, and probably many others, am immediately transported back to happy childhood memories of the excitement surrounding Christmas when I first beheld my own set of trains chugging along the tracks under the family tree. Each year many residents donate assorted Christmas figures to enhance the train's village.

Our community looks forward to resident Roger Leonard's annual dramatic reading of Dickens' *A Christmas Carol*, and our holiday concert by the Pondaliers always gets a packed house. To me, a swelling chorus of voices— sopranos, altos, tenors and baritones—singing in harmony represents a quintessential collective effort to achieve a beautiful sound by submerging the individual within the group. I always feel especially close to my fellow residents when we sing together as members of the Pondaliers, recognizing the months of dedicated rehearsals we have given to achieving a standard of performance that pleases our community.

If you want to see the exuberant spirit of our residents, join us on New Year's Eve when the ladies dress up and we put down our portable dance floor (paid for by our residents' Foundation Committee) in the Game Room. Resident Vivian Stoner, our indefatigable organizer, plays the role of D.J. and the administration provides champagne. Everyone brings enough finger food for an army and we dance into the wee hours of the New Year and then sleep late the next morning. WOW!

January brings our Super Bowl party and the informal betting pools, while February brings more dancing and fun at our Valentine's Day party, again organized by Vivian. This year in March we had a Cabin Fever Day, with many enjoyable activities to perk everyone up in hopes of an early spring, and in May, Vivian repeated her role as D.J. a third time in organizing a Spring Fling. Special events continue throughout the summer months when we can enjoy the large patio outside the Dining Room and especially the section covered by our new awning outside our Pub.

I must not forget to mention Halloween when half the residents dress up and the other half laugh and applaud us. The wait staff joins in the fun with costumes and masks, and a multi-generational spirit of tomfoolery prevails. Residents can also sign up to participate in a "trick or treat" event, where children of our staff and grandchildren of our residents excitedly go from door to door in a safe, enclosed environment. It would be impossible to say who enjoys this more: the kids or the seniors. I think it's probably a tie.

All these celebrations reinforce the strong camaraderie that I find to be so prominent a feature of my life at Woodland Pond and something that no marketing brochure can adequately convey.

The Bond of Shared Experience

With our frequently visiting young families, our young wait staff and the many young members of our administration and maintenance crew, we enjoy, as I've said, a multi-generational environment. However, I have discovered a small but rewarding aspect of my life at Woodland Pond to be a social history that we seniors share exclusively.

We remember gathering around the big radio in the living room (a Philco in my home) with our families and listening with rapt attention to our favorite radio programs. Of course, there were programs our parents liked and others strictly for kids, and then there were the ones we all listened to. Radio, using only voices, music and sound effects to tell any story, left the listener to fill in all the gaps with his imagination, picturing characters, places and events. For me, and perhaps for many others, radio was the foundation of our future creative lives.

WE REMEMBER: the advent of television— only in black and white; rotary dial phones with party lines, dirigibles, propeller planes and the coming of jets; girls wearing pigtails with ribbons and boys wearing knickers with the long socks always falling down; most men and just about all women wearing hats; ice boxes and washing machines with hand-cranked wringers; 78 rpm records that then became 33 and 1/3 long-playing records and then morphed into cassette tapes and finally CDs; when JFK Airport was called Idlewild and Muhammad Ali was called Cassius Clay; Saturday matinees at ornately decorated movie theaters where you could spend four hours watching all the short subjects, cartoons, adventure serials, coming attractions and news, added to the double feature, with admission prices ranging from ten cents to a quarter (and who, in their wildest dreams, could have ever guessed that at a future time in our lives we could re-watch these movies in our homes on large flat-screen televisions by inserting a tiny disc into a machine and pressing a button?); when doctors made house calls and penicillin replaced sulfa drugs; jitterbugging; the Automat; the names of popular movie stars, singers, sports personalities, politicians, religious leaders and Broadway shows of the 30's through the 50's; words and expressions that are no longer used (café society, stewardess, soda jerk, gas pump jockey, chip off the old block, behind the eight ball, a horse of a different color, a life of Riley, once in a blue moon, Kilroy was here) but were once part of our popular vernacular; old makes of cars now extinct (Studebaker, Edsel, Hudson, Packard, Plymouth, Nash); games that urban kids used to play (potsy, kick the can, ring-a-levio); and, of course, the effects of WW II on the military and civilian populations and, for some, the poignantly unsettling experiences of the Great Depression.

Yes, there are many memories both good and not-so-good that we share as a common bond that somehow reinforces our successful passage through life to the present and all the incredible scientific, technological and cultural changes we have witnessed and weathered in our generous span of years.

So whenever a group of us gathers in conversation and some aspect of the past comes up and someone might make a reference to Kate Smith, Sonja Henie, Walter Winchell, Lowell Thomas ("So long until tomorrow.") *Let's Pretend, The Shadow, Inner Sanctum*, Patti Page (the Singing Rage), Faye Emerson, Tom Dewey, Rosie the Riveter, The Ink Spots, Charles Atlas, Tokyo Rose, Gayelord Hauser, Tom Mix, Baby Snooks, John L. Lewis, Spike Jones and his City Slickers, *Easy Aces*, Joe Louis, Bishop Fulton J. Sheen, Pan Am, Ed Sullivan, Woolworth's, Adlai Stevenson, *Look* magazine, the hokey-pokey dance, the Dionne quintuplets, *What's My Line?*, *Carousel*, Howdy Doody, Mary Marten, Jeanette MacDonald and Nelson Eddy, Tyrone Power or Hedy Lamarr, everyone smiles with the glimmer of recognition and no one says "Who?" or "What?"

I find that there is another significant aspect to this background of shared experience. What to most people of succeeding generations is a part of history, read in books, was, for us, part of our lives and our **living** history. Climb aboard my memory train and let's take a brief trip back to those decades that evoke vivid images in our minds because we **experienced** them.

Many of us were born during the decade of the Great Depression and have personal childhood memories of WW II, with some of us having escaped from Europe as children and others having served in that war as young adults. This portion of our history is vividly reflected in the stories of **Wartimes Remembered.** At the end of that war we witnessed the transformational coming of the Atomic Age. Our rivalry with the Soviet Union ushered in the long period of the Cold War.

Remember how we practiced taking shelter under our desks in school rooms across America in the event of an atomic bomb attack? How naïve that was! The pre-pubescent boys in my class made up a snickering limerick: "Get under your desk and look to the sky—Get ready to kiss your ass goodbye." Okay, I admit it: I made up that limerick in my earliest stage of creative writing, but it became very popular with my classmates.

The decade of the fifties brought us the Korean conflict and the McCarthy hearings. A vast public sat transfixed in front of television sets, many with "rabbit ears," watching those hearings. Who can forget Joseph Welch's famous rejoinder to Joseph McCarthy, "Have you no shame sir? No decency?" James Dean, an idol of the younger generation, was tragically killed at twenty-four. Girls mastered the hula hoop and boys exchanged baseball cards.

In 1960 we saw the inauguration of the first American Catholic president and a First Lady who brought high fashion to the White House. The Cuban missile crisis had many of us believing that we were on the brink of all-out nuclear war and possible extinction.

As young adults with very young children, my wife and I were suddenly confronted with the shocking possibility of no future and our lives cut short. For that unforgettable week in October, 1962, when tensions mounted from moment to moment as the Russian ships with their nuclear warheads continued streaming towards Cuba, we huddled together with our babies, hardly sleeping, and tried to extract the fullest measure of love and comfort from each second. When the announcement came that the ships had turned around and the crisis had been averted, an overwhelming sense of relief flooded our lives, but, still, we recognized the perils of living in the nuclear age and resolved to live fully, and more consciously joyful in each succeeding day. Never, before or since, had we come so close to annihilation.

I'll bet that most of us remember what we were doing on November 22, 1963, when we first learned that President Kennedy had been shot, and then as this astounding tragedy unfolded, it was announced that he was dead. (Remember how Walter Cronkite's voice quivered and he had tears in his eyes when he made that announcement, clearly struggling to maintain his professional composure?) Numbed with shock, regardless of our political leanings, we suspended our lives for a period of days and participated in the nation's grieving rituals.

Compounding our astonishment was our witnessing the next day, via television, the actual shooting of Lee Harvey Oswald by Jack Ruby, and the incipient rumors of a communist plot, as confusion and doubt gripped the public. Who can ever forget the stoic dignity of Jackie Kennedy as she led the leaders of the world in that sad, solemn funeral cortege, and the "riderless" horse (with the stirrups symbolically turned backwards)? Perhaps the most indelible memory of all is that of little John-John, as the world called him, responding to his mother's prompting and saluting his father's casket.

Our living nightmares continued as we witnessed the assassinations of Robert Kennedy and Reverend Martin Luther King. Many of us felt our society was collapsing as tumultuous happenings seemed to be occurring everywhere, bombarding us at frequent intervals.

The decade of the sixties also saw a remarkable cultural revolution. How many of our current seniors had beards and mustaches and wore those bell-bottom trousers? I must confess that I did. My Columbia University graduate student ID card has me looking like D''Artagnan from *The Three Musketeers*, complete with shoulder-length hair and swooping mustache. At least I had the good sense (or inhibiting self-consciousness) not to participate in all the streaking episodes around campus that were a common occurrence.

To show how widespread and mainstream these affectations were, I maintained this tonsorial style while serving as department chairperson and assistant headmaster at an exclusive private prep school, as did many of the younger members of the faculty, with nary a remark or protest from the headmaster, parents or Board of Trustees. Indeed, many of them adopted similar looks, as did most of the students.

The student uniforms included white shirt, regulation tie and navy blue blazers embossed with the school's emblem for the boys, and uniform skirts and blouses or sweaters for the girls. From the neck down, they (and a lot of the faculty) looked conservatively respectable; from the neck up they (and we) were full-blown hippies. This was a cultural tide too huge to resist and we were all swept up in it.

Women wore mini-skirts, burned their bras, sported afros regardless of their ethnicity and confidently expressed their equality with men. The Beatles and Rock 'n Roll emerged supreme, and we took to the dance floor to gyrate wildly in new dance patterns where partners never touched and some people even danced alone.

Nudity was everywhere: on Broadway (***Hair, Oh Calcutta***), on campuses, in magazines and certainly at Woodstock during the famous four-day music festival and "love-in." The early death of Marilyn Monroe, a huge star of the mid-twentieth century, was a shock. Marijuana entered mainstream middle-class society, replacing cigarettes as a smoking habit. At my two *alma maters*, NYU and Columbia, you could hardly enter a men's bathroom during the break between classes without getting a contact high from the pungent smoke.

After WW II and Korea, many of us had had enough of war and openly challenged our country's participation in the Vietnam conflict. Not just college students but people of all ages protested through marches in cities, towns and villages across the country. For the first time my wife and I and many of our friends "took to the streets" to wage a citizens' battle against this grinding war. In exercising our right to assemble and to protest, we found strength in numbers. History now tells us that our voices and our presence at rallies and marches and our calls and letters to government officials and, yes, the unruly student riots across the nation's college campuses, all contributed to influencing President Johnson's decision not to seek a second term.

At that time I was already a Navy veteran, having followed in the footsteps of my father and grandfather (except they were officers and I was an enlisted "swabbie"). They had both served during wartime but my enlistment was in the halcyon span of years between Korea and Vietnam. My younger brother served in Vietnam as a helicopter pilot and bore the severe psychological scars for the rest of his life—one of the "walking wounded," as I frequently thought of him.

Many of us also exercised our constitutional freedoms as citizens to join in the heroic struggle of African-Americans for full civil rights, determined to eradicate Jim Crow laws and "separate but equal" practices, and to finally realize the full meaning of the sublime assertion (but really, at that time, only an aspiration) in our Constitution that "all men are created equal." Contrast that inspiring belief with Governor George Wallace's exclamation, "Segregation today! Segregation tomorrow! Segregation forever!"

The ubiquitous television camera captured the tumultuous struggles of so many brave men and women, black and white, confronting the seemingly overwhelming forces of bigotry and hatred. Suffering verbal abuse, physical assaults, attacks with fire hoses and even death, they steadfastly continued the inexorable march toward full equality as we, as a nation, examined our consciences and found a truer meaning of justice and equality for all.

The 1969 Stonewall riots in Greenwich Village, New York City, unleashed a force that few of us understood, but that would accelerate the gay rights movement at a faster pace than any other minority group's battle for equal protections and benefits under the law. Today, thanks to our relatives, friends and associates (and the politicians, celebrities and sports figures) who openly, proudly acknowledge being LBGT (Lesbian, Bisexual, Gay, Transgender), thereby bringing the issue home and making it personal for many of us, the majority of Americans are supportive of full gay rights.

We seniors have witnessed first-hand this swift and remarkable transformation in attitudes—what young people now take for granted. Perhaps only in retrospect can we who personally experienced all these seismic changes fully appreciate the historical impact of that turbulent (60's) decade we were living through. And let's not forget the triumphant capstone to that decade with Neil Armstrong's walk on the moon ("One small step for man; one giant step for mankind.").

In the 70's we were again transfixed by the Watergate hearings and the resignation of Richard Nixon, the first president in our two-hundred-year history to resign the presidency. Remember the foreign countries' embargo on oil and the subsequent shortages resulting in massive lines at the gas stations and soaring prices at the pump? Another entertainer icon, Elvis Presley, passed away at a premature age.

In the ensuing decades, wars continued to be part of our national profile: Granada, the first Iraq war, the second Iraq war and Afghanistan. We've seen the fall of the Soviet Union and the rise of

China, the fall of the Berlin wall and the rise of radical Islam, with "9/11" being the first successful, full-scale terrorist attack on the continental United States. And in less than a half-century the first IBM computer, mammoth in size and restricted in operational functions, had morphed into tiny portable machines—laptop, kindle, I-pod, I-pad, I-phone—with enormous storage capacity (thanks to the microchip) and undreamed-of capabilities, yet exquisitely simple to use (unless you're technologically challenged, like me, and can only master the basic functions).

Let's not forget my favorite, most user-friendly invention—the microwave oven. How would we divorced men, if you're clueless in the kitchen, have survived without it? Since half of all marriages in America end in divorce, I'm pretty certain that many men would join me in rating the microwave right up there with the microchip.

Our government, our businesses, our military, our global interactions and many of our personal functions now operate through a computerized world—perhaps the most remarkable transform-ation in any senior's life span of remarkable changes. I pay most of my bills, monitor my investments, do most of my shopping, find answers to perplexing questions, read the digital *New York Times*, communicate with friends, conduct committee business, watch streaming movies and write and format my books for publication, all via my desktop computer. When I sojourn in Puerto Rico, my handy laptop allows me to continue these practices.

Yes, we have lived through it all and have survived to share our memories of what I posit to be one of the most turbulent and fast-changing periods in man's history. Is it any wonder that references to these shared life experiences can enliven and enhance our daily discourse?

Getting About

I, along with many of our residents, continue to drive, but if the time comes when I no longer wish to have my own car, it's reassuring to know that Woodland Pond provides transportation—we own two small buses—for grocery shopping, religious services, visits to nearby malls and, most importantly, for medical appointments. A weekly schedule of designated days for different destinations helps residents plan their errands and make medical appointments.

All day Wednesday and on Friday morning, buses will take our residents to any destination of their choosing in New Paltz, Highland and Rosendale and then, at an appointed time, pick them up and return them to Woodland Pond. Monday and Tuesday are the designated days for medical appointments in Kingston, while all-day Thursday and Friday afternoon are designated for medical appointments in Poughkeepsie. Sunday morning is given to transporting residents to the church of their choice.

For local, state and national elections, our busses run a shuttle service to the voting venue and back to Woodland Pond, extending over several hours, thereby allowing all residents to continue exercising their cherished voting rights.

The buses also take us to numerous cultural events throughout the mid-Hudson area. To avoid parking hassles I always avail myself of our bus transportation to some play, concert or dance performance that our community, in a democratic way, has expressed an interest in attending. And wherever possible, we're usually driven to the front entrance, avoiding long walks from distant parking facilities. After any performance, I particularly enjoy the lively discussions that take place on the bus during our return home. Our freely expressed comments usually reflect a variety of critical responses to what we have just attended. Is this surprising with any group of seniors? I think not; however, it is stimulating.

Our bus drivers are extremely considerate and take great care of all of us. On many trips with our drivers Mike Ennis and John Hoey, I have personally witnessed frequent acts of kindness they perform with thoughtfulness and solicitude. We are lucky to have such caring professional drivers.

A Cultural Cornucopia

I frankly admit that I'm a culture junkie!

I have always loved live theater. My parents took me to see my first Broadway play, *Arsenic and Old Lace*, when I was six years old, and I've been hooked ever since. I saw my first opera (at the old Metropolitan Opera House on Thirty-Ninth street in New York City, decades before Lincoln Center was built) when I was nine, and attended my first classical concert at Carnegie Hall that same year, all provided by my parents. Since those early introductions, classical music and opera have always appealed to me.

Thanks to my former wife who was a professional ballet dancer before earning her PH.D. and becoming a tenured English professor, I learned to appreciate ballet (and cats, too).

Throughout my adult life, wherever I've resided, I've always availed myself of most cultural offerings. Now, as a resident of Woodland Pond, I happily find that I can continue to enjoy a rich cultural life, thanks to the many offerings that are available in the Mid-Hudson region (Newberg, Poughkeepsie, Rhinebeck, Kingston, Woodstock, etc.) and our convenient proximity to New York City.

Plays, concerts (both classical and pops) and ballet—mostly touring troupes—have become an ongoing pleasure for me and many of my fellow residents. Best of all, we are driven to many of these events, as I've mentioned, picked up immediately after the performance and whisked home. Who wouldn't enjoy such pampering? Residents are often given the opportunity to attend the simultaneous telecasting of operas from the stage of the Metropolitan Opera Company in Lincoln Center at the venue nearest to Woodland Pond. Again, no driving and no stress is what I appreciate.

For the years when my wife and I had season tickets to the Metropolitan Opera, it was always a hassle getting to Lincoln Center through the crush of Manhattan traffic and searching endlessly for some nearby parking space on the street or paying an exorbitant amount for a parking garage. Since our reserved seats were high up in the third balcony—we called it the nosebleed section—I spent most of the evening with my binoculars glued to my face in an effort to not just hear the mellifluous voices but to observe the dramatic acting. (Most opera buffs would agree with me that Maria Callas did not have a great voice but her acting was stupendous.) Now I calmly ride on one of our Woodland Pond buses to a nearby theater and watch everything on a huge screen as though I had the best seat in the orchestra. And at a fraction of the cost!

I like the Woodland Pond system for choosing the events each month to which we'll be driven. Gretchen Daum, our terrific Activities Coordinator (already praised in these pages and always deserving of more), together with resident

Ruth Kaplan who expertly chaired the Activities Committee until very recently, would compile a list of upcoming events across the area. At an open meeting to which all residents are invited, we vote on the events we'd like to attend. The five or six events garnering the most votes are then incorporated into the coming month's Woodland Pond official calendar and transportation is provided.

If I'm interested in attending some event that was not included (because it didn't gain a sufficient number of votes from the residents at the meeting), I can drive myself and take other residents who might wish to attend but don't drive. You will always find people who share your interest in attending additional offerings and who appreciate our informal car-pooling approach.

SUNY New Paltz, so convenient to us, is always offering interesting lectures, and its Communications Department stages full-scale productions available to the public—some of the many advantages of being located in the same town as a state university and having only a five-minute ride from our campus to the college campus.

Each month's official activities calendar usually includes a Lunch Adventure, where we visit an interesting restaurant in another location (beyond New Paltz). I'm especially grateful for these excursions since they help me expand my knowledge of, and growing appreciation for, this beautiful area which was totally new to me upon becoming a Woodland Pond resident.

It's comforting and reassuring to know that as I grow older and decide that I no longer care to drive, I will still have many opportunities to enjoy those cultural events that have been a pleasurable mainstay in my life I've heard many residents remark the same, and this is yet another advantage to living in Woodland Pond.

From my fellow residents I learned about a local excursion company, Adventures for Rascals, that offers frequent trips to Manhattan to see matinee performances of Broadway shows. On these excursions, my fellow residents and I drive to a local designated spot where a chartered bus picks us up and drives us directly to the theater where our show is playing. We're in Manhattan with plenty of time for a leisurely lunch. When we leave the theater after the performance, our bus is waiting for us to return us to our local drop-off spot. We then carpool the short distance back to Woodland Pond. Since I always found driving in Manhattan (even when I lived there) to be a stressful challenge, I'm delighted with this service and frequently sign up for shows.

John Sagan, the enterprising owner of Adventures for Rascals, offers extended trips to places of interest within the United States and abroad, ranging from a few days to a few weeks and usually escorted by him. The great asset of his packages is that they include transportation from our local areas to and from the designated destination (including airports when flying); thereafter, all transfers, accommodations, many meals, entertainment and gratuities are included in one price. You just relax and have fun.

Many of my friends at Woodland Pond have taken trips, both foreign and domestic, with the gregarious John and raved about them. I, too, am planning some trips with him next year, since I've been so pleased with my several Broadway excursions. I love leaving the driving to others whenever it involves congested areas like Manhattan or many hours of driving.

Speaking of driving, my recent acquisition of a two-seater hardtop-convertible sports car at the age of seventy-six caused a bit of a stir in our community, leaving some residents wondering what possessed me, at my age, to buy such an impractical vehicle. My explanation was simple. I love sports cars; I have always loved sports cars, as did my father, and I have always owned sports cars throughout my adult life. Some men play golf; some men hunt or fish. I drive a sports car (and the area surrounding Woodland Pond with its magnificent vistas and winding country roads is an ideal place to drive a sports car in the summer and fall with the top down).

To me, a car is an extension of my home, my personal space, an instrument of pleasure, and not just a conveyance for moving between point A and point B. I take great delight and pride in my home, as I do in my cars. I'm not trying to impress anyone. I'm just intent on enjoying myself to the fullest, and opinion be damned!

In my book *Infinite Gestures*, I include a short story called The Woman Who Thought She Could Dance that probably expresses my views on the opinion of others most accurately. In this story a working-class woman, uninhibited in her actions, demeanor and dress, marries into a wealthy family that is hidebound in their narrow social code and acutely concerned with what others think of them. They condemn this woman for her flamboyance and gaucheness, but it turns out that she and her husband are the only happy members of the family with a successful marriage, principally because they are indifferent to the opinion of other family members and society-at-large.

In the famous play (and the movie) *Auntie Mame*, the lead character says, "Life is a banquet and most poor suckers are starving." As long as I'm able, I'll continue to relish the offerings of life's daily banquet, be they large or small, with disregard for what others might think. I see incidents continually at Woodland Pond indicating that other residents clearly share my view, and their untrammeled exuberance continues to inspire me to extract the fullest measure of joy from each day.

Undaunted Courage

In becoming a member of a senior community ranging in age from 60's to 90's, I have witnessed something that has had a profound effect on me. Every day, in my interactions with fellow residents, I find examples of people who are facing the challenges of growing older squarely and courageously.

Let's face it: We all hope that we'll live to be at least one hundred, maybe a little frail but still healthy and in possession of all our faculties, and then pass away peacefully in our sleep. Right? Unfortunately, statistics demonstrate that this scenario is not played out for the vast majority of us.

For me, I find that my mental (psychological) age is usually about ten or fifteen, and sometimes even more, years behind my chronological age, and it takes some pretty dramatic events to reconcile the two. Here's one example.

When I was about sixty-five, I joined some friends, a couple, who were at least ten years younger than I, and we visited a new condo development that these friends were considering moving into. We toured the model unit but the wife wanted to see a larger unit and the sales representative, a man in his forties, pointed to a townhouse still under construction, with lots of debris scattered around it and a big mud hole directly in front of the porch.

Undaunted, the wife said she wanted to see the layout of the interior and grabbing her husband's hand she scampered across to this unfinished unit, with the salesman and me in hot pursuit. Being good athletes and addicted to daily gym workouts, the couple agilely leaped across the mud hole and landed on the first step leading to the porch.

The young salesman made a similarly graceful leap and landed successfully in the same spot. Now it was my turn. Having been a member of track teams as a runner, low hurdler and distance jumper in my far-distant youth, my mind still retained the image of my days when I sailed across extensive spaces with a single bound. Sadly, this mental image did not include the many pounds I had added to my figure in the intervening decades. Instead of my mental image of a gazelle, I should have pictured a water buffalo.

Without any hesitation, I hurled myself into the air, my legs scissoring forward in total confidence of an equally successful landing. Imagine my surprise when, the next second, I was ankle-deep in mud and, pitching forward, my body lay sprawled across the two steps leading to the porch. While I had the wind temporarily knocked out of me, I sustained no injuries except for some minor bruises to my arms and some major bruises to my ego.

It's situations like this that dramatically remind me of the passage of time and the adjustments one must make to the current condition of one's body. Things we did in the past with ease can suddenly become downright challenging in the present. Acceptance and adaptation are demanded.

Woody Allen once quipped that he had no fear of death but it was everything leading up to it that worried him. As the years flow quickly by, and our bodies change through the natural aging process and any day can bring some new ache or affliction, it is endlessly inspiring to me to see how my fellow residents confront these realities with unflagging optimism and unmitigated zest for living. They accept what is, but refuse to be bowed by what might be.

In all my days at Woodland Pond I have been acutely conscious of enjoying an environment that offers sterling examples of seniors whose affirmation of life imparts valuable lessons on how to grow old gracefully and intrepidly, and I feel blessed to have such courageous models of people living fully in the present, mindful of, but never cowed by, physical challenges. This positive spirit is pervasive in our community.

Pervasive Acts of Kindness

While Woodland Pond residents have come from different geographic areas, different backgrounds and different personal experiences, we have all committed ourselves to spending the rest of our lives here, and we are dedicated to making this both our home and a supportive community. To that end residents constantly extend themselves in innumerable ways to help and support one another.

When I was laid low for a few days with a bad cold shortly after I arrived at Woodland Pond, I received phone calls from neighbors inquiring how I was feeling and asking if I needed anything. I couldn't help but gratefully reflect on how different my current environment was from that of my previous condo where neighbors regularly ignored one another. Not to put too fine a point on their indifference but I honestly believed that if, for some unforeseen reason, I suddenly collapsed in the parking area, other residents, pulling up in their cars, would see me, say nothing and consider it an inconvenience to call 911 but reluctantly do so. There's probably a bit of dramatic license in this depiction (after all, I am a fiction writer) but not too much.

Here at Woodland Pond when residents with dogs become temporarily indisposed, they can always count on volunteers to walk and feed the animals. When I'm away in Puerto Rico for the winter, my neighbor Bill Harris takes care of my plants. Actually, it would be more accurate to say that Bill takes **better** care of my plants than I do. Neighbors are always offering to drive non-driving neighbors to different venues.

If a resident moves to Assisted Living, Memory Care or Skilled Nursing, all within our Health Center in a separate wing of our sprawling building, cards, phone calls, flowers and visits are demonstrations of support from caring friends.

We even have a Friendly Visitor Program, whereby residents in Independent Living volunteer to regularly visit residents in our Health Center.

Anne Smith, who has a cottage with her husband Ray, has a therapy dog that she takes to the Health Center once a week and visits those people who enjoy dogs and find comfort in a friendly dog's presence. Jean Hicks, another resident and my neighbor, likewise brings her beautiful miniature poodle, Brea, once a week to perform tricks for the Health Center residents. I have personally observed the joyful engagement of these residents with the clever, gentle Brea.

Here's another great example of our supportive community that I experienced first-hand. In the fall of 2012 the Foundation Committee, with the full cooperation of the administration, organized a special event that they called Kaleidoscope of the Arts and Sale, which featured all the arts and crafts of our residents: paintings, drawings, sculptures, photography, wood furniture, needlework, quilts, books, stationery, jewelry and assorted hand-made personal items. The event was open to the public and was a great success. Many items were for sale while others were just for display, but they all showed the diverse creativity of our community members.

I had planned to display several of my books for sale since residents had been purchasing them on the internet and I could offer the books at a reduced price, forgoing my royalties. Last-minute circumstances prevented me from being present at this event but two friends, Kathy Kelly and Vivian Stoner, who were manning a display table near the one I had been assigned, urged me not to cancel my book display and said they would take care of my table as well as their own. I returned to Woodland Pond two days after Kaleidoscope to find orders for fifty-seven books that my friends had taken. That night at dinner I treated each of them (and our tablemates) to a bottle of wine as a small recompense for all their extra work.

The prevailing spirit of generosity and caring was perfectly illustrated for me when a beloved member of our community, Nancy McBride, was tragically killed in an auto accident. I had known Nancy through our participation in the Pondaliers, the Play Readers Group and our hilarious games of charades, and had enjoyed many evenings at dinner with Nancy and her equally esteemed husband Doug.

Along with all the residents, I mourned the tragic loss of this charming and vivacious lady and attended her memorial service out of respect and appreciation for Nancy, to show my support for Doug and express my condolences to her family. What I witnessed at that service deeply impressed me as another example of the caring people who comprise our community.

In all my years of attending memorial services I have found that most elegiac testimonials are general in nature: what a good spouse, parent, friend, neighbor, etc., a person was! But Nancy's memorial service was, in my experience, unique because many people were eager to share **specific** acts of kindness that Nancy had shown them.

A young staff waitress who had lost two close relatives in quick succession tearfully related how Nancy had comforted her and had become a substitute grandmother. A man told of how he was reluctant to go for a battery of tests at a local hospital and kept putting it off until Nancy insisted on driving him there and then waited hours to drive him back.

Resident after resident related stories of Nancy's generosity in extending herself to them, as well as incidents revealing her great sense of humor that could lift a person's spirits. Their stories reminded me of a Sunday brunch I had enjoyed with Doug and Nancy. Nancy had selected a chocolate covered donut and, after consuming it with relish, said to Doug in a **mock** accusatory manner, "Why did you let me eat that donut?" Doug had a snappy response and we all laughed. Their breezy exchanges underscored their comfortable devotion.

Nancy's interpersonal skills coupled with her empathetic and giving nature and delightful humor had clearly left an indelible impression on all of us. For me, this one person seemed to encapsulate the loving spirit that is a hallmark of our community and is demonstrated every day in myriad ways, large and small. No brochure about Woodland Pond, I reflected, could capture this special dimension of our one-extended-family feeling.

I called Doug from my winter retreat in Puerto Rico where I was writing this personal history of my living in Woodland Pond and asked his permission to describe my feelings about Nancy's memorial service, which he graciously gave.

Shortly after Nancy's service, a call went out for volunteers to read the monthly newsletter and calendar of events to a small group of residents who were vision impaired. I volunteered and found as much joy in performing this service as the residents did in receiving it. When they mentioned that they had heard other residents discussing some of my books but they couldn't listen to any of them because none was on tape, I offered to read them selections from my three books of short stories. From there we proceeded to two of my novels (plus a preview of this book in manuscript form). We continue to meet every Saturday. A more appreciative audience I could not imagine, and I look forward to our get-togethers and the ladies' insightful discussion of my writing. You give and you get so much more in return.

One evening I was having dinner at a table for four. One of my table mates remarked that a neighbor was ill but a gentleman was walking the neighbor's dog. Another tablemate smiled and said that she repaired all the sweaters of that gentleman; the third table mate said that she had helped him with his garden. I sat there thinking that the circle of caring friends performing a thousand acts of kindness extended throughout our large community, immeasurably enriching our lives. I felt a surging pride in being a member of such a caring group. The standard for thoughtful, random acts of kindness was high at Woodland Pond, but I was inspired to meet it.

Lessons Learned

My residency at Woodland Pond has more than fulfilled all my hopes and expectations, and, through the example of my fellow residents, has reinforced or taught me many life lessons: courage and forthrightness in facing the realities of aging with an indomitable spirit and without losing your sense of humor or your zest for living; the joy of being bonded in a fellowship of seniors who offer friendship and, through their many acts of kindness, contribute unstintingly to the prevailing happy tone of our community; the security of knowing that no matter what the future holds, you will be provided for in a caring environment at a reasonable cost, in familiar surroundings, nurtured by friends; the exponential rewards in being of service to others; the strong desire we all share, no matter what our age, to continue growing in a stimulating environment with interesting and vital people.

When anyone asks me about my life at Woodland Pond, I can only reply with superlatives, but I offer some advice if someone is considering joining our community or any CCRC for that matter. Be sure to read all the available information and don't hesitate to seek clarification on any items that seem vague. Read the By-Laws, the Resident Handbook and the proffered contract thoroughly. Because this is a decisive life-change you're making, it might be wise to do as I did and consult a lawyer specializing in elder care to be doubly sure that there are no surprises in the future.

Without doing the necessary homework it's easy to misinterpret important aspects of the offering. I usually give an example of what I've observed with a few of my fellow residents who thought that upon entering the community, the monthly maintenance fee charged at that time would never change. That is definitely not the case. The monthly maintenance fee can be raised (or lowered) annually, subject to approval by New York State.

What doesn't change is when you might require greater care and be transferred from Independent Living to any of the three other units (Assisted Living, Memory Care or Skilled Nursing) in the Health Center at Woodland Pond. Regardless of the much higher fees normally charged for these additional services, if you opted for the Life Care offering when you became a resident, you continue to pay at the rate of the **current** maintenance fee for your apartment or cottage—a guaranteed savings of many thousands of dollars each month. You should also carefully examine the private health insurance you currently have, in addition to Medicare, and weigh this coverage against the Life Care insurance offered by Woodland Pond and other CCRCs.

It's equally important to understand fully what a Life Care policy does and does not cover—Woodland Pond's policy explicitly states all this—so that, at some future time when you might be in a vulnerable state, you and/or your family will understand exactly what are the responsibilities of Woodland Pond and what you could be responsible for. In my long-term financial planning I've made provisions for these possible out-of-pocket expenses while at the same time recognizing the major benefit of the Life Care plan in the future.

An ongoing discussion among many residents centers on what support systems are (or should be) provided in Independent Living. The administration usually responds to residents' questions on this topic by stressing that, while we are provided with some support such as the Personal Emergency Response System (PERS button) and a policy of a follow-up evening call when a resident has not been seen by the staff during that day, the expectation is that in living independently, we do not require the additional services offered in the Health Center.

While this topic continues to be debated, I feel that from the beginning, I had a full understanding of the services I could expect in Independent

Living by carefully reading all the information Woodland Pond provided me prior to my arrival. Residents, as a group, can always request more services but, in terms of a contractual obligation, we have no guarantee that these will be provided.

While the monthly maintenance fee for any Woodland Pond unit may, at first glance, seem steep, I made an interesting discovery. In the preliminary packet that Woodland Pond gave me long before I made any decision to enter the community, there was an exercise sheet asking me to itemize all the expenses I was currently incurring in my primary residence, including property taxes and home insurance.

I carefully completed the sheet, filling in all my current expenses, and was amazed to find that while the stated monthly maintenance fee for my desired Woodland Pond unit seemed quite high, the many items provided by Woodland Pond— such as heat, central air conditioning, electricity, water, food, grounds maintenance, snow removal, all exterior and interior repairs (unless caused by the resident through negligence or abuse), housekeeping services, garbage disposal, and transportation to a variety of medical, religious, entertainment and shopping venues—significantly reduced any difference between the cost of living in my condo and in my potential residence at Woodland Pond.

Other considerations quickly came to mind. While living in my condo I discovered a leak in the pipe leading to my washing machine. Although I was paying a hefty monthly fee for maintaining the outdoor area and communal amenities, it was my responsibility to find a plumber and pay for the repairs—in this case, a very hefty sum. If I were to encounter the same problem at Woodland Pond, I would merely fill out a Work Order and the leaky pipe would be fixed at no additional expense to me.

When I factored in the "special assessments"—money collected from each condo owner to cover any big renovations such as a new roof, or emergency repairs such as damage from storms, floods, etc.—over the years of my residency, the monthly cost of living was about equal to Woodland Pond's maintenance fee and I was getting so many more services for my money!

I'm never surprised by those things that occasionally surprise some fellow residents, and my strong recommendation is to take extra care to fully understand every aspect of the Woodland Pond contract before making any final decision. I bombarded Michelle Gramoglia, our excellent financial officer, with phone calls and questions, and she always responded promptly with answers to my total satisfaction.

If you're seriously thinking of joining our community, take advantage of the administration's offer to visit us for an overnight or weekend stay, free of charge. In interacting with our residents, I'm positive you'll find us to be a high-spirited, involved group of seniors who are happy to have arrived at Woodland Pond and would welcome you as a new neighbor.

Concluding Thoughts

In writing this brief (and, with apologies, occasionally discursive) history of my experiencing Woodland Pond, I will again stress that these are personal viewpoints offered voluntarily to pay tribute to the residents, staff and administration, all of whom contribute immeasurably to my daily state of total contentment. Despite my ongoing blissful state, I have no wish to present Woodland Pond as a Utopian society where harmony reigns and conflicts never emerge. No one who has arrived at a senior status would accept that depiction as anything but a fantasy.

I will state, therefore, that while this community turned out to be the ideal place for me, there are a few residents who seem soured on everything and appear incapable of deriving any genuine pleasure from life's daily happenings in their present environment. They often remain remote from the general population and our cheery hurly-burly, or they join groups only to cast a pall over any proceedings with ongoing negative comments. I found them easy to spot in the midst of our happy clan because they seldom or never smile. Fortunately, they're vastly outnumbered.

Experts in the field of gerontology say that as we get older, our fundamental personalities don't change; our basic traits just become more pronounced. Thus, I can only conclude that these few people have always viewed the glass as half - empty rather than half-full. Whatever painful life journeys have apparently caused them to see everything through a negative lens, I feel sad that they cannot embrace their dynamic, gregarious neighbors and be nourished and enriched by this caring and joyful community.

I have frequently heard from those residents who joined the community in the first months when Woodland Pond officially opened—they are considered the "pioneers"—that promises were made to them that were not subsequently fulfilled. While I must honor and respect their concerns, I entered the community two years after its opening, and must evaluate the effectiveness of the administration exclusively by how it kept its promises to me. Using that standard, I can find no instance of broken pledges or indifferent responses. When there might have been a few, short time delays, I took immediately steps to reinforce my requests, which were always handled to my complete satisfaction.

Despite my persistently happy state, until a short time ago I had a "pet peeve." As some point prior to my residency it was decided that, with the exception of a few public spaces, only artwork created by our residents would adorn the hallways leading to our apartments. The multifarious talents of many of our resident artists and crafts-persons were handsomely displayed about our complex, enhancing our environment and, I'd bet, stimulating other residents toward creative pursuits. However, given the size of our complex, there was a significant visual disparity between the halls that were adorned with these warm, creative renderings and those that remained institutionally sterile.

Whenever I strolled along a corridor that was displaying residents' works, I was mindful of the "homey," inviting atmosphere these created, while my own corridor and several others were devoid of any such touch. I understood that there had to be communal standards for publicly displaying art. However, since it seemed impossible to adorn all the corridors with residents' artwork, I felt strongly that the resident Décor Design committee should extend its guidelines and pass judgments on acceptable art and craft pieces from other sources.

I stated my view to Sarah Hull, our excellent Resident Services Director, and a short time later I was delighted to learn that the policy had been liberalized and loans or donations of artworks would no longer be restricted to those created by the residents. I then joined the Décor Design Committee and found the committee members to be discerning but fair in accepting pieces given by the residents for public display.

Encouraged by this change in policy, I purchased six oil paintings and donated them to the community. The donator (or, in most cases, lender) can determine where the pieces should be placed, and I had mine placed along my corridor nearest to my apartment. As a result of this new policy, many residents have come forward with artwork to be displayed in hallways, thereby giving our corridors a much more attractive and inviting ambiance.

When friends of my age or a little younger visit me and see my happy state of mind and marvel at the amenities I enjoy, as well as my very active lifestyle and my productivity level (three books and a play, in less than two years), they usually say that while they wish they didn't have the time-consuming, pressured burdens of home ownership, they're not quite ready to make a change.

To this kind of comment I immediately reply, "Nonsense!" Then I stress how a Continuing Care

Retirement Community like Woodland Pond is primarily designed for active, healthy seniors who, unencumbered with home ownership, want to continue to live independently while enjoying services and amenities comparable to a beautiful resort and feeling secure about healthcare resources in the future. Every day at Woodland Pond for me is like a holiday, and I'm sorry that I didn't move here earlier.

In a book published in 2012 titled ***Extraordinary Centenarians in America: Their Secrets to Living a Long Vibrant Life***, the author noted, "The people I talked to seek joy and find joy. They also were totally outside themselves and always thinking of others." It's easy to discover, as I did, that these qualities are exemplified in the Woodland Pond community on a daily basis. The caring nature of our residents reminds me of Winston Churchill's statement, "We make a living by what we get, but we make a life by what we give."

Whenever I leave Woodland Pond for any stay elsewhere, be it overnight, a weekend or my winter sojourn in Puerto Rico (which keeps getting shorter every year), upon my entering the driveway at the entrance of Woodland Pond, I'm always thrilled to discover how emotionally connected I am to my community and how happy, even excited, I am to be returning home. I've heard other residents express similar feelings, and perhaps that's the best testimony to the enriched lifestyle, zestful atmosphere and long-term security that Woodland Pond offers.

At the conclusion of Voltaire's satirical look at the world in his acknowledged masterpiece *Candide*, the central character, after viewing so many destructive forces subjecting mankind to hardships and misery, determines that he cannot face the world's problems with any optimism and will find a measure of peace only within a personal world created around friends and loved ones and the pursuit of one's private interests.

Cultivating one's garden is how Voltaire described this practical approach to happy living. I often think of this powerful piece of literature— actually a philosophical treatise disguised as a comic novel—as I go about my daily life at Woodland Pond. In this beautiful and stimulating setting I eagerly look forward to each new, rewarding day, grateful that after a long life blending both happy and tragic events in a wide, turbulent spectrum of experience, I have reached a peaceful and safe haven where I can continue to flourish, sharing laughter, learning, love and joyful living with my peers.

Afterword

Shortly before this book was being finalized for publication, our community lost a beloved member, Pete Johnston, who was the second friend I made upon entering Woodland Pond. I mentioned Pete previously in these pages as a retired editor of the **New York Times** who had served as the managing editor of the collection of our residents' war memories that was published as a book. Among those stories was Pete's own history of serving in the Army Air Force during WW II as a navigator. When his plane crashed in Italy, he was seriously wounded. The results of that crash affected his health for the rest of his life, but he never complained and pursued sports vigorously.

Pete left the **New York Times** to teach at Columbia University's Journalism School and later at the School of International and Public Affairs. He continued teaching until he was eighty-four because, as he said, he loved it. He and his wife, Jane, also a teacher and currently president of our Resident Council, had been married for sixty-four years when he passed away at eighty-nine.

I never saw Pete without a smile on his face and a perpetual twinkle in his eyes, as though his daily life held endless happy possibilities even as he faced increasing health challenges. In our conversations together, even a few days before his passing, he always expressed great joy in coming to Woodland Pond where he and Jane found so many new friends and a warm and stimulating community. We sat together in the tenor section of the Pondaliers and helped keep each other on the right notes. Everyone who knew Pete loved him for his warmth, his kindness and his humility. I especially enjoyed his droll wit. He was my buddy and I shall miss him keenly.

I deem it fitting to end my personal history with these comments about Pete, for all communities should be blessed with residents like him. At his memorial service, his family members, including five children, repeatedly spoke of how happy and energized he and Jane had been in their years together at Woodland Pond. In such a testament, coming at the end of a life when the truth is fully told, you have an unvarnished endorsement of the caring community that I take pride in calling my home.

CPSIA information can be obtained at www.ICGtesting.com
Printed in the USA
BVOW03s2029101113

335965BV00003B/10/P